WHAT YOUNG LEADERS NEED TO
KNOW TO DEVELOP THEIR INFLUENCE
POTENTIAL

By Alan E. Nelson, EdD

ISBN-10 1460961269
ISBN-13 9781460961261

Library of Congress Control Number: 2011907822
CreateSpace, North Charleston, SC

DEDICATION

This book is dedicated to you, a young leader. I want to apologize for older people who so frequently overlook your ability to influence and therefore don't really treat you like a leader. Even some of the best people still think, "Someday, you'll be a leader. In the future, you'll be a great influencer." We use the term "next generation" or "next gen" when you're actually now! You can make a difference now, not just later. You're not on hold. Leadership is the ability to get things done through people, and it's not confined by age, just our minds.

I know that this belief varies from family to family and culture to culture, but overall, we've done a terrible job identifying and developing people like you. I've begun an organization and hopefully a movement to change this. But even for me, it took half a lifetime of doing leadership development to realize the error of my ways. I don't underestimate how difficult it will be for corporations, countries, and cultures to change. But change we must, if we're to see the quality of effective and ethical leaders our world needs. We have a lot riding on you, so take your job of leading seriously. Practice now, when the risks are lower. Far too many of your older peers have practiced when the risks were high, and many have paid a big price as a result.

Naturally, I want to applaud the growing number of people around the world who are discovering KidLead and our LeadYoung training programs. I'm impressed with the high caliber of leaders who are embracing these resources and implementing them in their organizations and cultures. In the first three years since our official start, KidLead has become a global influence, even though we're highly decentralized, "lean and mean."

Thanks to Mark and Jennie Ross, an awesome couple who helped edit this book.

I also want to thank Lia Rodriquez Romero from Buenos Aires, Argentina, the artist who created the chapter graphics. The main character is depicted with a heart because this book is more about leading with heart. Anyone can read a book on leadership that focuses on the head (what we know) but true leaders combine what they know with character, intuition, and an inner sense of social influence. Leading with heart is difficult to explain or learn, but it's what great leaders do best. These characters are neither male nor female because leaders can be either gender. They also have various hues of shading, denoting the array of ethnicities and cultures of leaders. Lastly, the leader is ageless, recognizing that you can lead regardless of whether you're old or young.

As this book is read in various countries and cultures, our intention is to continue updating it in terms of what we learn about leading in different cultures. While the essence of leading is universal, what it looks like and how it gets done changes a bit from culture to culture because leading is about organizing people who vary in values, languages, and styles. But leadership is also about accomplishing things together that you can't as individuals, so, in that way, leadership is the same around the world.

TABLE OF CONTENTS

A MESSAGE TO YOU
FROM THE AUTHOR

Dear Young Leader,

Thanks for picking up this book. I hope you enjoy it. More importantly, I hope you see how important you are to the future of society. Rarely will you ever find a serious book on leadership that is written for people ages 14 to 25. Leading young is quite different than older leading, but unfortunately, most leadership experts focus only on older adult leaders. That's sad because you have so much to give. You're in your formative years as a lifelong leader, and how you develop now will impact how you lead later, not to mention provide you with a ten- to twenty-year head start on other leaders.

I've led as long as I can remember. My earliest memories are during my first school years when we'd run outside at recess and the other kids would ask, "Hey, Alan, what are we playing today?" I'd pick softball, soccer, or occasionally (American) football, even though the teachers would tell us "no" if they caught us tackling. Most of the time my leading was a positive, but sometimes it wasn't. I got a few low grades in conduct for being a class clown. My leadership abilities weren't always productive, and they didn't always sit well with adults, who didn't appreciate me stealing attention from them in class or at home, where expressing opinions or a strong will were considered rebellious and thus quashed.

So it only made sense that I'd lead later in my life. I led in the social nonprofit sector for more than 20 years. But as early as college, I had a growing fascination with what it is that makes certain people more influential than others. I wondered how certain people got to be presidents, CEOs, and world and local leaders. When John Maxwell, the famous leadership author, hired my wife, I offered to drive him to his speaking engagements so I could learn from him. I started studying leadership formally, getting a doctorate from the University of San Diego. I started collecting leadership books, having more than 700 in my library, not to mention writing a few myself, along with hundreds of articles on the subject. I guess you might say I became a bit of a leadership junkie.

Because of my passion for the subject, by midlife (age 45) I wanted to focus solely on developing other leaders, but unfortunately, anyone who wanted to make a living doing this pretty much had to work with adults. Stick your head inside most executive training programs and you'll see that more than 90 percent are between the ages of 30 and 55. Leader developers typically become corporate trainers, executive coaches, or consultants, hired by companies to invest in their up-and-coming executives. The problem is that in the decade or so I'd been doing that, I realized that adults don't change very much. I didn't see how the investment in expensive training programs resulted in significant differences. The older people get, the less they tend to change. Therefore, a little change costs a lot of time, money, and effort.

I began wondering what it would be like to take the same kind of leadership training and "age size" it for leaders while they're adaptable. That began a three-year process of designing and prototyping the first executive-caliber training curriculum for preteens, called LeadNow. We later launched a nonprofit in the US, called KidLead Inc., and begin certifying trainers to use these 50 hours of active learning training in schools, civic groups, and faith communities. The program is now global.

Business people talk about ROI: return on investment. This is the rate of return you receive on your money. For example, if you invest $100 at a 5 percent rate of return, that's an OK return. But if you get a 50 percent rate of return, that's amazing. When you start learning leadership skills early, you have many more years to gain experience and improve. Plus, you don't have much to unlearn, a big challenge for older leaders who are more set in their ways. I'm dedicating the rest of my life to investing in young and very young leaders, because I've discovered a rate of return far greater than investing in adults. A growing number of others are catching this vision, realizing that the best hope for our organizations, communities, countries, and the world is to identify and develop young leaders, while they're moldable, not moldy.

To be honest, part of my motivation for doing this was personal. By midlife, I realized I'd not become as good of a leader that I thought I could be. I hadn't reached my potential. I wondered what it would have been like if someone had tapped me on the shoulder and said,

"Alan, I think you've got leadership potential. I'd like to invite you into a special training program to develop that." So hopefully my failure, of sorts, can be your success.

While our first focus was on 10- to 13-year-olds, because of their unique stage in life, we also knew that we couldn't stop there. We wanted to expand the span of leadership development from preschool through college. We've identified four stages in a young leader's life. Each is different, requiring unique strategies and methods to learn leadership effectively.

This book is specifically for ages 14 to 25 (the last two stages). Because you can think conceptually and handle complex topics, we want you to get a head start. Throughout history and still in some cultures today, you're considered an adult around 14. But we've prolonged the time between childhood and adulthood, to better educate and prepare you for life. Unfortunately we tend to see people your age as young and immature. Adults think, "Someday you can do great things with your life."

I disagree. You can do them now! That's what this book is about. It's about discovering that young leaders can do amazing things. You're bright enough to understand these essentials. Over the years, as I've worked with preteens I've come to the conclusion that young leaders can often learn these principles better than adults because they have so few lessons to unlearn and they have less to lose in becoming self-aware and admitting what they're learning. Humility is a vital ingredient for learning. Overconfidence closes our minds to better ideas.

Although you could read and understand most books on leadership, they're written for adults. LeadYoung is specifically for your age and stage in life. I've found that leaders are generally pretty smart people and I've no doubt that with a little bit of reflection and hopefully some interaction with others, you'll learn a lot from this book. I've not "dumbed it down" because you're young. I've tried to be conversational, because that is how leaders talk to each other. I'm focusing on specific skills and principles that will give you a head start in leading and will prepare you for further leadership reading and development. This book is a part of our LeadWell and LeadStrong training programs. It's the reading portion of a primarily learn-by-doing program. Because we have more participants involved in our LeadWell teen program, most of the illustrations refer to school settings.

So whether you're reading this book on your own or as part of our concentrated training program, I applaud you. Good job. You're creating a way of thinking and acting that will help you change the lives of people and the organizations you'll serve. I hope you keep in touch and spread the word about our work around the world. I'm convinced that society has yet to see its finest influencers. You're on your way to becoming one of them.

Believing in you,

Alan E. Nelson, EdD
Monterey, California
Check out www.leadyoung.org

THE BETTER THE START, THE STRONGER THE FINISH.

SECTION 1

UNDERSTANDING THE GAME

When I turned 16, I bought my very first car with my own money. It was a 1968 Ford Galaxy 500. (Come to think of it, that's also what I paid for it, $500.) I loved that car. I put the keys on a ring and twirled them like a big shot when I was hanging out with my friends—"Oh yeah, I drive. In fact, I have my own car." It wasn't cool like a Mustang or Camaro, but it was mine. There's just something about sliding the key into the ignition of your own car and turning on the motor. Vroom!

We're going to give you some keys to drive your leadership. You can't twirl them on a ring, but they'll take you a lot further than that Galaxy 500 took me. The first section of this book will introduce you to 11 important principles about being an effective leader. We could talk about dozens and hundreds of principles, but we picked the ones we believe are most important to you as a young leader. That's why you won't get a lot of them in other leadership books, which are typically written for older leaders.

- **Chapter 1** defines leadership, because hardly any books do that, yet everyone throws around the term as if they're talking about the same thing.

- **Chapter 2** answers the question, "Who can be a leader?" The answer probably is not what you think; at least it's not what most adults think.

- **Chapter 3** introduces the three primary roles in the leadership process: Leader, Influencer and Participant. Get them wrong and you'll mess up your leading.

- **Chapter 4** helps you identify when leaders are actually leading. I've never read this idea anywhere, but it's very important when you watch a leader.

- **Chapter 5** is about identifying leaders around you, because if you don't know who they are, they can work against you. We'll show you how to tap their influence.

- **Chapter 6** shows you how to lead people on your level (laterally), which is unique because most books are about leading down.

- **Chapter 7** introduces you to leading up, leveraging the influence of those with more power than you. This is a secret weapon for young leaders.

- **Chapter 8** is called "'Sitch' Leading" because most leaders lead the same way in all situations ("sitches") and therefore make a lot mistakes. We teach you four styles.

- **Chapter 9** will show you how to design your own leadership projects so you can get experience, even if adults don't give you any.

- **Chapter 10** provides ideas for finding leadership mentors who can help you get a head start.

- **Chapter 11** teaches you how to give and receive great feedback so you can improve personally and also help your team get better. Very few adult leaders know how to do this well.

So hold on to your seat—we're giving you the keys to drive your leadership.

If you are reading this book as part of the LeadWell training program, you'll be expected to read a chapter in Sections 2 and 3, per concept you're focusing on in your current training module. Section I is good to read anytime. If you're not reading this as part of the LeadWell teen training program, then enjoy it all right away.

CHAPTER 1

DEFINING LEADERSHIP

OK, just for fun, I challenge you to lay this book down for a moment and write your definition of leadership. You're probably saying, "Come on, I just started." But trust me, this will make the rest of the chapter more interesting. In fact, let me give you some space to write your definition. Go ahead. There are no right or wrong answers, and writing in books is fine as long as they're yours. If this isn't your book, then get a piece of paper or on a computer and write your response.

My definition of leadership:

Did you do it?

Chances are, your definition has something to do with being a good person or helping people do things together. If so, that's great. Most people think very positively about leadership when they're defining it, but leadership can also be used for evil.

Leadership is about helping people work together to achieve what they could not or would not as individuals. Leaders are people who use leadership, who get it going. Leadership is a social skill that can be used for good and bad, but by itself it's neither good nor bad.

Sorry, I'm getting ahead of myself. So why is it important to define a term that you're using? The biggest reason is simple communication. Let's say my wife sends a text message that says, "Pick up some bread." That's pretty simple. Get bread. I'm out. But if you think about it, that text could mean a lot of different things. I could go to the bakery and buy croissants, banana bread, pumpkin bread, or any number of pastries. I'm assuming it's more about grocery store bread. But even then, there are a lot of options. Should I buy whole wheat, white, multigrain, Texas toast, potato, sweet, French, pumpernickel, Hawaiian, rye, sesame, or cinnamon? There are so many options. Any one of these may cause her to shake her head when I pull it out of the bag and put it on the kitchen counter when I get home.

I need specifics. "Get a loaf of whole grain, wheat bread." That helps. Then I only have half a dozen brands and prices (I live in the US). Oh well.

Since KidLead has become a global program, I've begun doing more international travel. I'm fascinated by the various religions in countries. Most cultures talk about God, but they have different concepts of God. If you're talking to a Christian, Jew, Muslim, Buddhist, or Hindu, you'll hear some common words, but they have different meanings.

The same is true for leadership. A lot of people talk about leading and leadership, but very few define what they mean when they use the term. At one time, I had more than 700 books on leadership in my personal collection. Very few of them defined the term. Over the years, I've discovered that leadership means a lot of different things to people. There seem to be three categories that nearly all definitions fall into:

- **Personal leadership:** *Being a responsible person, having good self-esteem, being a good citizen, possessing character, being confident, being self-motivated, taking a stand for things that you believe are right.*

These are all valuable qualities. We want everyone to be responsible and make good moral and ethical choices. We want to work around people like this, don't we? We want to go to school with people like this. But personal leadership, as defined here, is quite different than other types of leadership. A lot of people like to call this leadership because these are the qualities we want to see in our leaders. We want them to be people of character who we can trust and who are responsible. An irresponsible leader disappoints a lot of people. A leader lacking character will eventually ruin an organization. But you can be a good person and not be a leader.

Although I'd hope that 100 percent of people could possess this type of leadership, reality says that some people have things that keep them from this, whether it's an emotional problem or a really bad family experience that makes living a responsible life very difficult.

- **Managerial leadership:** *Heading up a class project, teaching a class, managing a shift at a factory, owning a small company, overseeing a small group of people who work together.*

This is a more refined definition of leadership than the previous category of personal leadership. An individual who leads this way has more defined skills. This person may be a schoolteacher who is in charge of an entire class of students. This could be you when you're helping fellow students accomplish a group project. Your job is to get everyone to work together for a very specific task.

A lot of people can learn how to be managerial leaders. Probably 70–80 percent of people can provide a modest level of leading when it comes to leading or co-leading others in smaller projects. Quite often, you see people who use other talents in combination with this type of leadership, who only lead in that setting. For example, a person who is good at teaching may lead in the classroom. A physician may lead her team in a medical office. A mechanic may lead three or four others in a garage to fix cars together.

Managing is different than leading. It's a type of supervision, being in charge and working with others, but the process of managing a project is different than leading people in a project. Getting people to do the same thing over and over is different than helping them embrace change and giving them a vision and purpose for what they're doing.

- **Organizational leadership:** *Leading a larger group of people, casting a vision for a preferred future, bringing about change in an organization, getting people to accomplish together what they could not as individuals.*

This definition is more complex than the first two. The number of people who have the ability to lead organizationally is quite a bit fewer than the others. Naturally, we hope that organizational leaders will possess personal leadership skills. As we said, we want them to be ethical, responsible, and possess self-esteem so they aren't proud or self-centered. We assume that people at this level could also lead managerially, whether it's in a classroom, on a specific project, or in something that requires simple leadership abilities, such as suggesting something to do with friends after school or stepping up to get your group to clear a restaurant table after you eat.

But this book is about organizational leadership. This is a more complex skill set, when the leader strives to provide vision, initiate change, and help people work together to accomplish goals they weren't originally pursuing or with a significantly better approach. This is not the type of leadership that everyone can do, or at least do well. Some people don't like it when I say this, but it's true. There's no research anywhere that supports the idea that everyone can become this kind of leader; but some people can. You may want to take the free, online assessment on the KidLead.com website or better yet, have an older adult who has observed you in social settings, take it on you. This Social Influence Survey helps identify young leaders and those with an aptitude for learning how to lead more effectively.

Here's our definition, one more time:

- **Leadership is the process of helping people ac-complish together what they could not as indi-viduals.**
- **Leaders are those who get leadership going.**

When people start talking to you about being a leader or leadership, ask them for their definition. "What do you mean when you use the word 'leadership'?" This helps you know if you're talking about the same thing, or at least better understand what they mean. For the rest of this book, we'll be using the previous definition. This helps us understand leading as a unique social skill set. It's not something that comes easily, and also isn't so generic that we confuse it with just being a good person or an upstanding citizen. By defining it more narrowly, we stand a better chance of learning what it means to lead and hopefully becoming a much better leader.

Leader Reflections:

1. Why do you think it's important to define leadership?

2. How is the definition I provided different than what you've thought about leadership?

3. How is this definition different than what other people think of leadership?

4. Based on this definition, how do you think of your-self as a leader?

CHAPTER 2

WHO CAN BE A LEADER?

I've got to be honest with you. Some of you may not like reading this chapter, because in it I'm going to tell you that you have limitations, and few people like hearing that they have limitations. In fact, I've found that some people get downright angry when they hear what I say in this chapter. I've had many adults get mad at me when I tell them what I'm about to tell you. Ever have someone angry with you? It's not fun, is it?

Perhaps this chapter's title should be, "Who is apt to be a leader?" If you're from the US, as I am, you're likely to get irritated with the idea that you can't always be what you want to be. After all, you're young, and if you have loving parents, you've been told that you can do whatever you want to do in life. Well—reality check—you can't.

Don't get me wrong. You can do a lot in life; you can do amazing things, I believe, but not whatever you want. Here's why; we all have limitations. At the time I'm writing this chapter, I just turned 52 and I'm a bit overweight. So let's be honest. If I wanted to play in the National Basketball Association (NBA), it's not going to happen. In fact, forget my age and weight. I'm just not wired to play. I never had the speed and coordination to play professional ball. I could dream all I wanted. I could go to camps and shoot baskets all night, but I don't have the capacity to play in the NBA.

Does that mean I can't be successful in other areas? No. Does that mean I can't be happy, fulfilled, and productive? No. It just means I can't play in the NBA. In fact, out of all high school basketball players in the US, only 4 percent go on to play in college. Of that, only 1 percent will get a basketball scholarship to a Division 1 university. Of them, Only 1 percent will go on to play in the NBA. So what does that tell us? It says that we're all wired to be winners, but not in the same area. It also tells us that we'll be most successful if we find out what it is we're good at or have the ability to become good at, and then focus on those areas.

What does this have to do with leadership? Well, based on how we define leadership, people possess varying abilities of learning how to lead. What we've found in working with students ages 10 and up is that only a small percentage possess a strong ability to learn how to lead—about 10–20 percent. More are able to learn how to lead at a lower level of effectiveness. As we get older, we gain more life skills that can sometimes substitute for more natural leadership talent.

We have people helping us develop leadership training for kids, ages two to nine. They tell us the same thing—certain kids just seem to have a natural ability to lead. Others are artistic, athletic, academic, and people oriented, but not leadership oriented. That's OK when you understand that the creator of the universe gave civilization leadership to help us all use our gifts more effectively. The power of teamwork is that it allows us to use our strengths and skip our weaknesses. Because leading is a small piece of the big puzzle, we don't need many leaders; a few can help the rest use their abilities together.

We don't have to pretend to be someone we're not. We don't have to fake it if we're not good at leading. We used to call people pretending to be something they weren't "poseurs." There are a lot of leader poseurs, people pretending to be in charge and know how to supervise, who don't know what they're doing.

How Are You Smart?

Harvard University professor, Howard Gardner, wrote a book several years ago called *Multiple Intelligences*. He realized that typical IQ tests and most schools measure only two types of "smart:" math/logic and language. Gardner realized that a lot of really talented people didn't always do well in school, but they could still be very successful. He discovered there are at least eight types of smart, people can be. For example, they might be art smart, meaning maybe they're really good with music, painting a picture or sketching a scene. Others are body smart, or have what is called kinesthetic intelligence. Perhaps they can run fast, pitch fast, or kick a ball through a goal.

Another type of smart is called interpersonal. These people are good with other people; they get along with them and get them to do things they wouldn't normally do. Some of these people are salespeople, others are entertainers, and a few are leaders. These people don't know why they are the way they are. They don't study their subject, but naturally understand what others don't.

Through the years of working with young leaders, I've seen a lot of really academically smart—"book smart"—kids. They get straight As and brilliant report cards. But usually they aren't the best leaders. We respectfully refer to it as the "geek factor." Their book smarts don't translate into people smarts. They can't seem to get their peers to buy into their ideas or organize others to follow them. That's okay; it simply means that whether or not you're book smart has little to do with whether you're good at leading. When you study intelligence, talent, and other abilities, you're likely to come out similar findings. If you plot everyone on a graph, a small number would have a lot of talent. Quite a few people in the middle would have a modest or low amount of talent. And then another small group at the end would have very low to no talent. Another way of looking at leadership ability is in this graph.

General Population Leadership

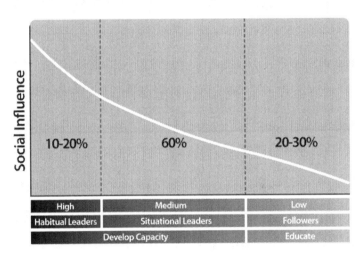

People on the far left of the graph have a strong aptitude for leading. They are what we call habitual leaders, because they'll always look for situations where they can lead. It might be a gang, an athletic team, a club, or a business, but these people almost can't *not* lead. That can be a problem when you don't need a leader, or the leader is a bad person, or when more than one leader tries to compete for dominance.

People in the middle of the graph are situational leaders. They can learn how to lead if needed, but they don't enjoy it and tend to get stressed when they are put in charge for long. This represents a lot of people. Most organizations need a certain amount of these people. In a large company, you need some really strong leaders who'll help the entire corporation operate and give vision to the rest, but you also need a lot of people in between to oversee smaller projects.

Sometimes I use numbers to describe leadership capacity. A 1 would mean very low capacity, 2 is low, 3 is medium, 4 is large, and 5 is very large. On a 1–5 scale, how would you rate your capacity? If you're a Starbucks fan, think of leadership capacity in terms of their cup sizes. They have short, tall, grande, venti and trenta. If you buy a tall cup of coffee, you want it full, because you're paying a lot for that drink. If you buy a venti, you want it full as well. No matter what your capacity, the goal is to reach it.

In life, a "grande" leader who is full can outlead a "venti" leader who is only half full. That's because the venti isn't living up to his potential. Maybe he's lazy or has never had anyone train or develop him. Wasting your potential is a sad thing. Our goal at KidLead and LeadYoung is to help identify leaders' potential and then provide resources that help them develop their full capacity.

The right side of the graph represents people who possess very little leadership capacity. There's nothing wrong with this; it's just not their thing. Just as some people are terrible at sports, others stink at art, and many (like me) are lousy at math; that's simply how we're wired. We can be successful, but rarely where we have low capacity.

THE QUESTION ISN'T HOW SMART YOU ARE, BUT HOW YOU ARE SMART.

The best thing for people on the right half of the graph is to learn what their gifts are, find good leaders, and serve on their team. They should learn how leadership works so they can avoid following bad leaders. If everyone had even a basic understanding of leadership, the Adolf Hitlers and terrible leaders of the past wouldn't have had as many followers. If a leader doesn't have any followers, he's not a leader.

Should you feel bad if you're not an organizational leader? Absolutely not. Chances are you can do things that most leaders can't. Success in life is a matter of using what you're good at to benefit others. If leading isn't your "thing," that's okay.

But what if you think you have intelligence in the area of leadership?   You'll do better if you work at improving your leading instead of merely relying on what comes naturally. Just as professional athletes work hard to develop their talent, and great musicians practice hour after hour, young people with leadership aptitude should intentionally work on their skills. That includes reading leadership books (as you are); going through programs like LeadNow, LeadWell, and LeadStrong; and interacting with other leaders who can mentor and teach you.

Seth Godin wrote a book called *The Dip*. In it, he said people who are really good at what they do have to go through a lot of work and pain to develop their skills to the point where few can achieve what they've accomplished. Godin says that people who are great are quitters. That's right—but they learn where to quit. They don't keep working at things in which they can't excel. They discover what they are good at and enjoy doing. As you read this book, you'll start seeing whether or not you're wired to lead. We will help you reach that potential. You can do great things with your life, leader or not. But if you're wired to lead, this book will show you ways to develop your potential.

FREE Social Influence Survey

Someone said, "What's your favorite word?" Answer, "Free." Over the years, we've developed a helpful tool for measuring a young person's aptitude for leading, called the Social Influence Survey (SIS). It's free. You can take it on yourself and better yet, have a couple people who've observed you in social settings take it on you. The survey consists of 25, multiple choice questions that you answer online. This tool is modeled after more complicated executive assessments, but is designed to reveal the ability to learn how to lead by revealing current ways that you're trying to lead. Just go to www.kidlead.com and click on the "Leadership Assessment" menu tab and then select the appropriate one. The SIS won't guarantee you will or won't be a leader, but it's a great place to start uncovering your leadership potential.

Leader Reflections:

1. Why is it important to consider a person's capacity to lead?

2. How did this chapter change the way you think about leading?

3. What did you learn from completing the Social Influence Survey on yourself?

4. What can you do to reach your leadership potential (in addition to reading this book)?

CHAPTER 3

LEADERSHIP ROLES

When people don't understand how leadership works, even good people can end up following bad leaders and doing things they'd normally never do. As we said, leadership is accomplishing together what we would not or could not as individuals. Leaders are individuals who get leadership going. So when unethical people become leaders, bad things are bound to happen.

Three primary roles operate in nearly every leadership situation. We'll label these as "Leader" (L), "Influencer" (I), and "Participant" (P). An easy way to remember this, at least in the English language, is LIP, the "kiss" of leadership.

L - Leader

The **L** is the role we're primarily talking about in this book. This is the person or persons most responsible for getting people to work together toward a common goal, whether three people or three hundred million. Sometimes the Leader is in an official position, such as a king, president, or prime minister. Usually, a leader is in more of an informal role, such as a gang leader, soccer team captain, or playground organizer.

People often compete for the role of **L**. That's why there are political campaigns, because certain individuals want to be the top Leader. Sometimes potential leaders fight and the winner gets to be the Leader. This fight may be physical, political, or of talent and ability.

I - Influencer

The **I** is a person who is not the main leader, but is still influential in terms of persuading people to think or act in certain ways. In some companies, this would be known as a middle manager, a person who oversees a group of people within a company. At other times, the **I** is a person who either doesn't have strong leadership potential or who doesn't want the responsibility.

Let's say that a CEO of a company is also helping his daughter's softball team. The CEO has a lot of power in the company, but when he puts on the assistant coach uniform during softball practice, his influence goes down significantly. He knows how to run a large company and supervise a lot of people, but he's an **I** on the softball team, because either he doesn't know a lot about softball or doesn't have the time to run the team.

Most organizations have any number of **I**s. Large organizations have many. These are people who possess less influence than the **L**s. They are important to leadership because the larger and more complex an organization becomes, the less Leaders can accomplish what needs to be done. Leaders can harness the **I**'s influence to get things done more effectively.

The reason for understanding the role of an **I** is when you need to get things done, there come times when only having Participants isn't enough. Understanding the role of an **I** is also important when you're a Participant or an outsider. This person can make introductions to the **L** in an organization. They can connect you to people with more influence when you are new.

For example, when I'm introducing KidLead's leadership training curriculum to an organization, sometimes I don't have access to the organization's Leader. I'm perceived as just another salesman, or the **L** doesn't have time to risk hearing about something that may not be of value to the organization. That's when I try to find an **I** in the organization who can meet me and then, if it sounds interesting, can introduce me to the **L**.

When I meet a Participant of an organization, I know that it's probably not a good use of my time, because that person will have to find a leader for me to meet and I'll end up doing the same presentation multiple times.

One way I find a leader in a school is to ask, "Who should I talk to about leadership development among your students? Who oversees this type of program in your school?" If the answer is not the Leader (principal/headmaster), chances are I'm going to discover an Influencer. This isn't always the case, because sometimes the Influencer has the top position and the Leader is someone else on staff or a volunteer.

All Influence Isn't Leadership

Sometimes we confuse people in charge with Leaders. I know this sounds odd, but just because a person oversees an organization doesn't mean that person is a **L**. All fathers are men, but not all men are fathers. All leaders have influence, but not all influence is leadership.

Let's say that we have a line called Influence:

____|_____|_____|_____|_____|_____
personal administrative managerial **leadership** inventor/creator

- **Personal influence** has to do with an individual's ability to influence others simply by being present. Followers have influence in their role, although it's a different kind of influence than leadership. A customer in a store may submit an idea that creates an improvement. The comment had influence, even though the customer did not lead.

When our three sons were kids, they liked McDonald's. My wife and I weren't very excited about eating there. But even though I drove the car, we often ended up at McDonald's. Our sons weren't steering, but they were influencing me. You've done that same thing to your parents, no doubt.

- **Administrative influence** organizes things in terms of keeping records, following guidelines or rules, and managing resources. Take for example an office administrator, supervisor, or treasurer. Each oversees certain tasks and people. They have influence. But keeping the rules or following someone else's vision or guidelines is different than leading.

- **Managerial influence** is being a manager in charge of things, someone who is more apt to help people keep moving in the same direction they're heading, versus helping them change directions. A manager is often in charge of a class, or team, or section of a company, but managing a project is different than leading it, in the way we've defined them.

- **Inventor/creator influence** is at the other end of the influence line. These are people who influence us by what they create, whether it's a rock star, software inventor, or best-selling author. They influence us, but not by organizing people to work together as much as by personal creativity.

- **Leadership influence** is a different kind of influence. You can be influential in life without being a leader. Just because someone is in charge, fills a position, or has an important-sounding title, that doesn't turn him or her into a leader. This may be a difficult thing for non-leaders to accept, but it's important for us to realize if we are to separate leadership from other types of influence.

P - Participant

A **P** is the backbone of the organization, because without people actively involved, you don't have a leader, you just have a person who thinks he's a leader.

Ps sometimes get a bad reputation because they're not leaders, but that's unfortunate. There are two kinds of **P**s: high value and low value. What makes a **P** a high value is understanding how leadership works and getting involved in the process. When a **P** is ignorant of what makes a leader good or bad, he has a lower value to the group or organization, because he follows without thinking. Another thing that makes a low value **P** is a lack of involvement. When he is lazy, doesn't care, or is self-centered, he won't help the team achieve.

On the other hand, a high value **P** is a person who understands the leadership process, uses her gifts and talents to add to the team, and is motivated to help others succeed. High value **P**s are vital to effective leadership because without them, you won't be able to accomplish much.

A smart **P** is a person who understands what it is you're striving to accomplish, and is willing to use his talent and time to help accomplish the goal. Most of the world consists of **P**s. A good **L** is able to identify **P**s who are smart and can add something beneficial to the organization. They're valuable, so a good **L** tries to find them and treat them well so they'll be a part of the team.

An ignorant **P** is a person who either doesn't know what the goal is, or is willing to follow a bad leader. There are a lot of low value **P**s in the world; they don't follow well and they keep the organization from being productive.

One of the things we train on in our leadership program is how to follow, because when a Leader doesn't know how to follow well, that person can cause problems. A good **L** knows how to lead, influence and participate, and when to do each. All of these are important within the leadership process.

Leader Reflections:

1. List one person who is a Leader in your school or organization.

2. Name a person who is an Influencer in your school or organization.

3. Name a person who is a Participant in your school or organization.

4. What do you think about the idea that all influence is not leadership?

5. Why is it important to know all three roles in leadership?

CHAPTER 4

LEADERS VS. LEADING

What's the Difference?

Other than one word being a noun and the other a verb, what's the difference between a leader and leading? People frequently confuse leaders with leading. For example, the leader in this graphic isn't leading at the moment. He's relaxing with his dog, perhaps thinking about playing sports or going to a movie, the same as any non-leader. The best way to learn about leading is to practice it yourself and watch other leaders, to see what they do when they lead. But watching a leader when he's not leading won't help you learn how to lead well. There's quite a bit of confusion on what it is that leaders do, because we fail to distinguish when they are and are not leading.

My son plays baseball. I just went to one of his games where the opposing team used the old "hidden ball" trick. There was a runner on second base. The pitcher acted like he was throwing the ball to the shortstop, who was on the base. Everyone pretended that the pitcher had overthrown the ball, turning toward the outfield as if watching a loose ball and the players running after it. Actually, the pitcher hadn't thrown the ball. The runner on second base, thinking the ball was loose in the outfield, started running toward third base. The pitcher then jogged over to tag out the runner, because the ball was hidden in his mitt. The runner was out.

Unless we identify who leaders are and when they're actually leading, we'll be like the runner who got out. We'll misperceive what it is leaders actually do. We may think leading is one thing, when it's not. We may believe that if we just follow or watch the leader, we'll discover what it is we need to do and then try to copy it. As a result, we'll waste a lot of time and energy, and we'll end up deceiving ourselves. One more time, let's determine who leaders are before we analyze when they're leading.

Oops, Maybe Not a Leader

Over the years, I've come to the conclusion that there are typically three categories of people who get mistaken as leaders: popular people, position holders, and smart people.

Let's start with popular people. Because of our work with young leaders, we're sometimes asked to provide training for student councils. I'm also a frequent writer for *Student Leadership Activities*, a magazine published by the National Association of Secondary School Principals. This periodical is sent to people in US public schools who work with students selected for leadership roles. Generally, about half of the people who get elected to student councils aren't strong in leading. They're just popular.

Popularity is an influence, but it's different than leadership. Naturally, you can be a leader and popular, but when you're popular and not a leader, it usually means that you're not strong at organizing and getting people to work together on a task. The ability to cast vision (a preferred future that motivates people to commit), handle conflict, and solve problems is a combination unique to leaders. When popular students discover what it means to lead, they usually don't enjoy it. One reason is that leading sometimes causes you to lose popularity because you have to make difficult choices, hold people accountable, and focus more on the task than being liked or having fun.

I know it sounds like I'm being hard on the idea of popularity. But when you talk to these people, they'll often admit that although they frequently get picked to lead things, they don't enjoy the pressure. As adults, these people frequently go into jobs such as sales, entertainment, public relations, and hospitality. These are places where they can use their people skills and likability, but don't necessarily need to lead things. Therefore, keep an eye on distinguishing between leaders who are popular and people who are merely popular.

Another category people confuse with leadership is position. Just because a person has the title of manager, vice president, or even president, doesn't mean that this person is a leader. You ask, "How can a person get promoted to a position of leadership if he isn't really a leader?" It happens all the time. The primary reason is that organizations resist change, even though they may need it. Organizations often reject people who try to change them, labeling them renegades, "boat-rockers," troublemakers, malcontents, and "black sheep." They even are called disloyal. This is unfortunate because when an organization needs to change to improve or even survive, someone who wants to change it is often more loyal than a person willing to leave it as it is or just make tiny changes. Therefore, people who won't create much change frequently get promoted to positions of authority and power, and the rejected leaders often end up starting their own organizations or finding a place where they can truly lead, where their ideas for change are welcomed.

Someone who has a title, position of authority, or a place on an organizational flowchart isn't necessarily a leader. There may be power in the position, but a position does not make a leader. When non-leaders fill positions of power, they often underutilize it and thus waste the opportunity.

One reason that non-leaders are selected for certain positions is because they're good at what they do and get promoted to a position of prominence. Unfortunately, the position doesn't require the same skills that got them there. For example, a salesman great at selling may get promoted to regional manager. But as the manager, instead of selling, he's supposed to be leading salespeople. He may be great at selling, but terrible at developing others, so now he's in a place where he won't be effective. In education, a teacher who is great at teaching may be selected to take the place of a retiring principal. People assume that if you're good at teaching, you'll make a great principal, but that is not true. Many schools are "led" by managers, administrators, and teachers who are good at what they do, but not at leading. They're not bad people; they just aren't good at creating change and helping the organization improve significantly.

We've found that in schools, many teachers perceive the students with the best grades as leaders. We've also noticed that the top students academically are frequently not strong leaders, as we mentioned earlier. These individuals are brilliant thinkers, but they don't know how to get their ideas accepted by others. Their social skills often lag behind their IQs, so that they have less influence among others. Henry Ford, founder of Ford Motor Company, was famous for saying, "I hire people who are smarter than me." That's the sign of a good leader.

I'm not saying that top students are not leaders. I'm saying that just because you're a good student doesn't mean you're a leader. Most leaders earn/receive above-average grades. They're smart, because leaders have to understand difficult situations, and they process a lot of information well. But book smart isn't the same as people smart. A leader has to be people smart to succeed at getting things done through people.

In addition to being smart, some people are perceived as leaders simply because they possess exceptional talent. On an athletic team, it may be the strongest pitcher, or the best kicker, or the fastest running back, or the most accurate shooter. In music it may be first-chair trumpet or violin, or a best-selling recording artist. People who possess exceptional skill and talent are not necessarily organizational leaders. While they are in the lead in their fields, they are really just ahead of everyone else, not trying to get everyone else to work together toward a common goal.

Leaders Aren't Always Leading

Let's start with an obvious leader: your country's president, king, prime minister or ruler. This person is frequently leading. That means working as part of a group to solve problems, casting vision for the future, and helping people work together to accomplish a goal. That is what leaders do. But some of the time, this leader is not leading. This person may have kids, and at times is parenting. The same individual may be married, so some of the time is being a spouse. In other situations, the person is eating, sleeping, exercising, and administrating, all of which are quite different than leading.

Let's say you have an opportunity to spend a day with this powerful person. You'll have 24 hours to follow him or her through the course of a day, like a shadow. Obviously, you'll learn some things about leading, as you see how the leader acts in situations where he or she is leading. But leading is a specific skill set that you use in situations. Yes, leaders should eat well, exercise, take showers, and invest time with their friends and family; they need this for their mental, spiritual, and physical health. But these activities are not actually leading.

Therefore, if you want to learn how to lead, try to determine when the person is actually leading, when he is in a situation where he is wearing the "leader hat." This will help you understand when you need to lead. You'll have a better sense of what is expected of you in the moment. Leaders need to know when to lead and when to do something else.

We call a person who is good at leading, who leads as part of a good portion of her life, a leader, even if she is not leading at the moment. The inverse may be true as well. You may know someone who does not lead consistently or who lacks this skill. Yet, in a specific situation that person may be leading. Look for a setting where a problem needs to be solved with a group of people. Notice when people lack direction and someone initiates a workable solution. Watch for individuals who step up to resolve conflict between people because intervention is needed. These are examples of leading. Even though these people may not be thought of as leaders, they may be leading. Even though you may not be an athlete, chances are you can throw a ball. Even though you'd never think of yourself as a cook, you can follow a recipe and fix a meal.

Here's my point. I hope you become a lifelong learner of leadership. I want you recognize who leaders are, when it is they are leading, and what it is they do as leaders. This will help you determine whether or not they're doing it well. As we analyze leaders while they're leading, we can learn from them. We can get better.

Leader Reflections:

1. Describe in your own words why it's helpful to determine when a leader is and isn't leading.

2. Describe an example of a leadership situation where you can actually observe a leader leading.

3. Which of the three categories of misperceiving leaders (popular, talented, position) did you find helpful?

4. What do you think about the idea that non-leaders often get promoted within their organizations? How can a leader avoid promoting non-leaders to places of leadership?

CHAPTER 5

IDENTIFYING LEADERS AROUND YOU

Why Should I Identify Other Influencers?

OK, now that we've gone over some mistakes people make when trying to identify people who have the ability to lead well, let's take a look at some of the signs and indicators of those who possess strong leadership aptitude. By aptitude, we're talking about the ability to learn how to lead. Obviously, there's a connection between learning how to lead and being able to lead. Why is it important to identify other leaders around you? The answer may not be obvious.

The main reason you want to identify leaders around you is because they have influence too. That means they have the ability to use their influence for or against you. Leaders frequently get themselves into trouble because they overlook others with influence and underestimate how another influencer can work against them. One way they work against you is simply taking more energy and resources. They get more people to follow them. At other times other leaders can work against you if they see you as competition or disagree with what it is you're trying to accomplish.

Let's say you're on your school's student government and you're trying to do a campus-wide program to get everyone to recycle. Typically, you'd plan the strategy and have relatively modest response. After all, everyone is busy with other things, so you'd have marginal success and wish that it had gone better. You think, "Oh well, that's life." But if you really wanted to be shrewd, you'd figure out who the other leaders were at the school. You'd look at the sports teams, the student clubs, and the informal networks. Then you'd individually go to these people and explain why this program was important, and you'd request their help in forming the plan and getting the message out to their group. Chances are, the results would be far more successful, because you identified other influencers who weren't on the student council, but who were leaders.

A reason why leaders fail to identify other leaders is because, typically, leaders don't naturally hang around each other. When you think about it, most social circles have their own leader or a few individuals who influence the rest of the group. That's what leaders do, influence people. But since leaders are typically busy with their own groups, they don't hang around each other. That's not good or bad, it just is.

Leader Indicators

By now, if you've taken the Social Influence Survey, you are familiar with a variety of ways that reveal leadership ability. But here are eight of the most common indicators of leadership aptitude, so you can analyze people you meet. You may notice a few of these in people who aren't strong leaders, but when you see several, you can assume the people are leaders.

1. **People listen to them.** Don't confuse "talking time" with "being-listened-to time." Just because a person talks a lot, doesn't make that person a leader. Sometimes, leaders are quiet. But when you're in a group of people, notice people's body language. When a leader speaks, heads turn, people turn their body toward that person, and they look up from whatever they are doing to pay attention.

2. **People seek their opinion.** An opinion leader helps others determine what they think about an idea. Therefore, when a leader has been quiet, others will ask the leader for his/her views on the topic. Kids

running out on the playground at recess will say, "Jack, what are we going to play today?" Jack picks the activity because his friends see him as the leader. These individuals also get noticed more than others when they're gone. "Hey, where's Josie today?"

3. **Others pick them to lead.** Some of you have been selected by your peers or adults to be the captain of your athletic team, run for class president, or to lead a class activity. If you interview older leaders, you'll find that most of them had this same experience when they were young. People intuitively sense who they want to follow or be in charge, so certain people get picked a lot to do things like this.

4. **They have a lot of opinions.** In many cultures, this is not appreciated by adults. Therefore, when young leaders give an opinion, they may be ignored or told to be quiet. Unfortunately, this makes them question their ideas and devalues how young people add to society. We're not talking about the chronic complainer or constant talker. Leaders have ideas on how to improve, organize, and solve things. Learning how and when to share these effectively is important, but to do that, they usually need practice, which means they'll irritate people at times. Adults often don't understand the value of young people's thinking. That's unfortunate.

5. **They've been accused of being bossy.** Having opinions is one thing, but telling people what to do and how to do it often comes across as bossiness. You can see this behavior in young leaders, as early as ages two and three, when they're telling their preschool buddies where to put the toys, what they're going to do next, or what role they have as they play pretend. Although certain personalities are less bossy than others, bossiness is typically an indicator of leadership aptitude.

An exception to this is in Asian cultures, where children are conditioned to respond with compliance, especially when parents are present. Even as teens and young adults, parents dominate home life so that young leaders often feel very restricted. What we find in Asia is that young leaders are good at getting friends to follow their ideas through more subtle ways.

One friend may suggest to the group, "Going to the mall would be fun." No one jumps on the idea so he brings it up again. Then someone affirms the idea so the leader says, "Oh yes, that would be a lot of fun, wouldn't it?" Gradually, others start suggesting they might like to go and the quiet leader finally says, "I think that's a great idea, everyone. Let's do it." The strategy is more of a persevering focus on the idea instead of the individual, but it was the leader who subtly promoted it among the group until there was consensus.

6. **They've gotten in trouble for being a disruption.** Most classrooms aren't very leader friendly. When you have teachers trying to control 20-40 students on average, they aren't very appreciative of those who distract others. Therefore, these people periodically get sent to the principal's or dean's office. They end up doing extra push-ups because the coach didn't like it when the team laughed at their jokes. Although all class clowns aren't leaders, many young leaders are able to steal attention from adults in charge. Non-leaders who do this are merely irritating to their peers. Again, this quality isn't as prevalent in Asian cultures, where this type of behavior is typically punished, beginning in early childhood.

7. **They're goal-oriented, ambitious.** Playing video games isn't a bad thing, but leader-type people usually aren't satisfied facing a screen hour after hour. They have ideas. They pursue projects. They chase dreams and tend to be self-motivated. The inner drive that makes leaders good at getting things done and achieving also keeps them from monotonous activities and mindless tasks. Leaders generally aren't lazy; they're active and tend to keep a lot of things going at any one time.

8. **They're likable.** Although it may sound kind of simple, when we surveyed teachers about students who were influencers, we discovered an overall likability factor. Sometimes this was described as good looks and dressing well. At other times it was explained as

being nice to others and confident. Certainly there is a charisma factor that causes us to like being around these people.

The bottom line is that a leader is a person others follow. If a person thinks she's a leader, but people don't follow, then she may not have a strong aptitude for leading. Certainly, none of us leads all the time, but if someone exudes a number of these qualities, leading is a strength.

Periodically, you'll find people who didn't demonstrate these qualities as a young person, but developed them later in life. Frequently this is because of a dominant parent or sibling at home. If a family member doesn't let a child lead, or verbally or physically intimidates her when she tries to lead, chances are she'll withdraw and sit on her leadership abilities. We see this a lot in certain family cultures (like mine as a youth). Sometimes even in groups of close friends, stronger leaders subdue the rest so other leaders don't develop their potential.

As we mentioned, these indicators also vary somewhat from culture to culture. For example, in Thailand, children and female teens are often expected to be quiet. You won't find many who are bossy or opinionated, or at least who are willing to express themselves assertively. We see more outgoing behaviors among young female leaders in the US. (We're learning a lot about young leaders as our work and research expands globally. We'll try to update this book and other sources as our experience grows.)

Being able to identify other influencers is an important part of leading well. You want to know who are your potential allies and competition. This will empower you in leading laterally, as we'll talk about in the next chapter.

A quick way to assess a person's leadership aptitude is to take the Social Influence Survey (SIS) on that person. Again, go to the KidLead website (http://www.kidlead.com) and you can do that for free. Answer the questions with the other person in mind, but you'll want to click the "Parent" button as a responder, so you can see the results; otherwise the results won't come to your e-mail address.

Leader Reflections:

1. Why do you think it's important to identify other influencers?

2. Who comes to mind as you read the eight leader indicators?

3. Which of these leader indicators do you see in yourself?

4. Take the SIS on yourself or someone else to give you a better sense of how to measure leadership aptitude (the ability to learn how to lead).

CHAPTER 6

LEADING LATERALLY

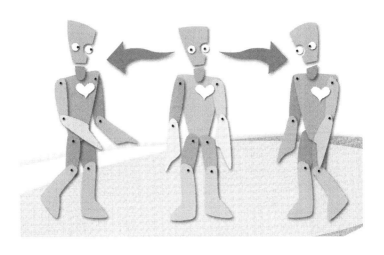

Influencing Peers

A peer leader is another influencer who has similar social strength and organizational power. Perhaps it's a fellow member of your student government, the president of a club at school, or co-captain of a sports team. Lateral leaders could also imply friends who do not see you as a leader, or perhaps a sibling. You may not have any official authority over this person, or for whatever reason, that person may not want to be led by you in a typical manner.

Hardly any books on leadership talk about lateral leading, yet it's at work in nearly all organizational settings, small or large. Lateral leading is not about leading down (followers) or leading up (superiors); it has to do with the horizontal influence. Because of your age, you're more likely to experience lateral leadership than many adult leaders. Developing this skill will take you far as a young leader and an older leader. The reason is that whenever there are people with similar influence, they can help you or work against you.

Another reason you need to understand lateral leading is because when you get into larger organizations, higher leaders often value those who have the ability to get along with each other and understand how to negotiate limited resources, while supporting the overall vision. When lower leaders don't get along and squabble, this becomes a burden to the leader and may affect your ability to lead up. Think about how parents get upset when their kids are fighting. Higher leaders feel similar frustration when mid-level and lower leaders can't get along.

Regardless of your age, you need to be savvy about leading those who are on a similar social level as you. Because you have fewer formal channels for leading, it's important for you to be effective at lateral leading.

Common Mistakes Leaders Make

Because we typically think of leadership in terms of influencing followers, we overlook the importance and challenge of leading laterally. Here are three of the most common mistakes leaders make:

1. **Misunderstanding the direction of influence.** It can go up, down, and sideways. If you don't know who has the greater influence, you'll make a lot of mistakes. When dealing with other leaders, you need to estimate if that person has more, less, or similar influence as you. When I teach at the Naval Postgraduate School, I'm familiar with rank, where power often comes from the position you hold compared to others. But most of the world is not as structured as the military.

   Over time, you'll be in roles where you'll do far more leading down than leading up or laterally, but the way to get to that point as a young leader is to emphasize the other directions. Here's the deal, when you're good at leading up and laterally, you'll be a far better leader at leading down.The reason is because you'll help your team members get more resources, power, and support than your peers who only try to lead down.

2. **Failing to estimate the influence strength of lateral leaders.** Imagine a game of tug-of-war, where you have your team on one end of a big rope and another leader and team on the other end. Now imagine a few more ropes coming out of the center, each with a leader and team on the ends. Everyone is pulling, trying to get the other teams to come their way and

avoid being pulled themselves. That's a mental picture of what's going on between various groups trying to acquire resources like people, money, time, and attention. When you underestimate the power of other leaders, you'll get pulled in directions you don't want to go, or you'll fail to get what you want. You may complain that it's unfair, and act as if there's nothing you can do about it, but you're not helpless. They may be feeling the same way about you and your influence. By understanding the influence of others, what they want, and how you might work together, you gain power to accomplish your team's goals.

3. **Trying to compete against other lateral leaders.** You can see lateral leaders as potential friends, or you can treat them like enemies. When you do the latter, you start competing with them. You may win short-term victories, but over time, other leaders will team up against you. Even though your goals may compete against each other, you're far better off sharing your common ground than making them mad.

For example, let's say your club and two others are vying for use of the same meeting room at the same time at your school. If you go over the lateral leaders' heads by meeting with the principal, you may get the room, but you've also lost credibility with the other leaders. That's what we call "winning the battle but losing the war." It would be better if you met with the other club leaders and tried to negotiate a win-win outcome so that you either agree to share the room or agree to adjust your schedules. This takes more time and energy and may cause you to lose a few small goals, but you've avoided unnecessary tension where these leaders use their influence against you.

Effective Lateral Leading

Here are a couple suggestions for how to effectively lead laterally. First, you'll want to approach a leader on your level with a sense of respect and honor. Naturally, we want to do this with all people, but it must be very obvious when leading laterally. If the other leader feels that you are speaking down to him, he'll be irritated or even offended, and working with him from that point on will be difficult.

Second, strive to create a connection with this person before you need to negotiate something for your team or as a leader. Establish a friendship, even if it's a mild one. Creating rapport with each other is an important part of working together. Once you identify who these other leaders are, strike up conversations with them. Meet to get to know them. Wave and smile when you walk by them in the hall, and call them by their name. Let them know that you're friendly and that you like and respect them.

In the US, people sometimes refer to this as the "good-old-boys club," because men who were friends often gave each other favors as leaders. But this was because they had become friends. They did things together other than merely meeting to discuss leadership issues. When you're on the outside of these social circles, you may see them as unfair. When you've done your work to build friendships with other leaders, you're really just being smart. Obviously, this is more difficult with some people than others, depending on your age, gender, personality, or in some cultures, social class (as in India); but this is important to do.

Third, lateral leading is different because you go into meetings with a need to figure out a win-win. Think in terms of what the other leader needs or wants, and how you can help them accomplish it. You'll also need to consider how the other leader can help you accomplish your goals, but realize that your goals may need to change a bit. You have to consider yourself an equal, not higher or lower, like in other leadership situations.

The better you become at leading laterally, the more effective you'll be as a leader, because you'll be helping your team gain influence from sources. As your lateral leaders become more powerful, they'll often help you as well. For example, if one of your current fellow leaders eventually becomes the CEO of a large organization, he or she may hire you or your company, or open doors that you would not otherwise have open to you. The lateral leader has become a higher leader, so that your leading-up potential becomes even more powerful than typical leading up. We'll talk about leading up in the next chapter.

Leader Reflections:

1. List four people who are lateral leaders to you.

2. What groups/teams do they lead and how might you lead laterally with them?

3. Why do you think leading laterally can be more difficult than leading down or up?

4. What other benefits could come from leading laterally, at least in your area of leading?

CHAPTER 7

LEADING UP

Which Way Is Up?

Nearly all books on leadership are about "leading down." By that we mean a leader organizing and directing followers. But unfortunately, when you're a young leader, you have fewer opportunities to lead that way. To gain experience as a leader and to get things done in an adult-oriented world, you'll need to "lead up." By this, we mean influence people who have more power, influence, and resources than you. It probably sounds a bit ironic that you can lead people who are stronger or even better leaders than you, but you can. In fact, this happens a lot. Sometimes leaders don't know when they've been led from below, because a person who is good at leading up is subtle.

Think of influence as water. Gravity causes water to flow from high to low places. Leadership power moves from strongest (highest) to weakest (lowest). So when you're interacting with a stronger leader, you need a special strategy that defies social gravity, so you can tap into the stronger leader's influence. Leading up has to do with influencing people with greater power than you, as part of your leadership strategy.

For example, let's say that you're the president of your band. You want to put on a fund-raiser that will in-volve the student body, alumni and the community. Your goal is to raise money to buy new music stands and more instruments. But your school board has determined that because of financial cuts, every fund-raiser has to be ap-proved by them, and in addition, anything that is likely to generate publicity in the community needs their approv-al. So for your event to happen, you'll need to persuade the school board that what you're going to do is impor-tant and that it will benefit the school, both financially and in public relations. You can do the typical approach of making a presentation at a school board meeting, but leading up means you'll want to consider other angles.

You may want to learn about each of the board members. Who has kids in the school? Who is the strongest influence among them? Who has concerns about your idea and who loves it? These are all questions you'll need to ask so that you know how to approach your presentation, or better yet, how you'll meet with each board member individually to cast your vision and address their concerns before your formal presentation to the entire board. You discover that one of the two strongest board members is a former band member and loves your idea. You even find pictures of him in an old school yearbook and make a copy to show him when you meet. As you get this leader to understand what you're doing, he also shares a couple of ideas that will benefit your event.

When you make your formal presentation to the board, you already have this leader's support, which in turn, influences his peers (leading laterally). The school board votes to approve your request. That's leading up, because this same board could have voted against your event and thus halted your progress.

How Do You Lead Up?

When you're young, don't hold a powerful position, or have a lot of credibility, chances are, you'll need to lead up if you want to get certain things accomplished. Three words determine your plan: what, who, and how.

- **What?** Before you try leading up, you need to answer the question, "What is it we want to accomplish?" If you don't really need to go after the influence of others who are older or stronger than you, then you won't need to lead up. Leaders are typically busy people, and they will want to know exactly what it is that you're trying to accomplish and what you need or want from them. Therefore, have a clear idea of what is important so you can communicate well.

- **Who?** When you've determined what it is you want to accomplish, start thinking of who has the influence you need. This isn't always an easy question to answer, because you may not know who it is. In the example we used, the school board was pretty obvious. A similar situation may include meeting with a teacher, principal, or superintendent. Discovering "who" may be as simple as asking people, "If we want to do _____, who do you think we should talk to?" Formal networks are a lot easier to discover than informal networks, such as friendships and unofficial leaders.

- **How?** How are you going to connect with this person? It may be as easy as setting up a meeting. If the person doesn't have time to meet with you, it may be as simple as knowing the person's work schedule so you can "happen" to run into him after work. You then walk with him from his office to his car, allowing you to casually introduce yourself and explain your idea. This can lead to another meeting to better present your plan.

Another approach is to find a gatekeeper. Imagine a leader surrounded by a tall wall that keeps out people. But these walls have gates, guarded by individuals who have access to the leader. Most leaders have official and unofficial gatekeepers. An official gatekeeper may be a secretary or staff member who handles people seeking the leader's attention. An informal gatekeeper may be a friend, family member, or even a neighbor. Developing a relationship with a gatekeeper can be an important step for accessing the leader.

A gatekeeper friend can introduce you to the leader indirectly by bringing up your name during a round of golf. A staff gatekeeper may be able to help you directly by getting you on the leader's meeting schedule. In the world of sales, salespeople are nice to receptionists and administrative assistants because they know that these people have the ability to schedule meetings with the decision makers. How do you plan to contact the leader and how do you plan to introduce your idea to her in a way she'll be willing to say yes?

Be Careful

Young leaders need to realize that although there is a lot of potential for good in leading up, it can also work against you. If you try to go around a person to get what you want, the person you avoid may stop you because they're mad that you went over their head. For example, let's say that you needed to get your school's principal to approve your event request. But because you didn't think he'd approve it, you went to the school board or to the superintendent, your principal's boss. Even if the board or superintendent says yes, now you've made the principal your enemy. You may get to do your event, but the next time you want to do something, the principal may say *no* because you went behind his back to get it done. Plus, he can make your work difficult as well.

History is full of stories of people who took risks going over the head of certain leaders and then paid a price for it. You need to be very smart and strategic in how you do this. You don't want to make enemies with influencers because they will use their influence against you.

Another thing you want to avoid when leading up is letting the leader feel used or manipulated. If you aren't truthful, or if you're just using the stronger leader without offering anything in return or thinking of her interests, the leader may not like it and therefore say *no*. A single rejection may not be a big deal, but if this leader now sees you as lacking integrity or credibility, she may say *no* in the future, avoid you, or even warn other leaders about you. This is what we refer to in the US as being on a leader's blacklist. That means the influence and power you wanted to work for you is actually used against you. You want to avoid making enemies of people with power.

A third reason to be careful is related to what we talked about in the last chapter, "Leading Laterally." If you're good at leading up, peer leaders frequently get jealous and try to work against you, because you've done well tapping into the higher leader's influence. You can see a similar thing happen in families, when one child seems to be better at getting her way than the other siblings. Dad or Mom may unintentionally start playing favorites, so that her siblings begin alienating her. They may even gang up against her and make her feel unloved because of the way she gets the parent to favor her.

When this kind of thing happens among leaders, the leader who has benefitted from leading up will also need to do a good job leading laterally. Otherwise, gaining from one leader may cause you to lose things you need from other leaders.

In summary, the ability to influence those with more influence is a very important skill for young leaders. In fact, it may be just as important as leading down. Not only will your followers and team members be impressed if you're able to help them gain access to resources that older people control, but stronger leaders will appreciate you and possibly give you other opportunities, whether it is a job, introductions to leaders they know, or just ongoing support. Leading up is not easy, but if you learn it early, you'll be well on your way to being a person of influence and getting things done, which is the bottom line of leading well.

Leader Reflections:

1. How would you define leading up in your own words?

2. Why do you think leading up sometimes gets a bad reputation?

3. Can you think of an example of leading up as a student or young person?

4. Think of a current project or challenge and who you might tap (lead up to) who has more power than you?

5. What are the risks of leading up, and have you seen this happen?

CHAPTER 8

"SITCH" LEADING

One Size Doesn't Fit All

When you shop for clothes, you try to find something that fits. When you find an item you like, chances are, you'll go to a fitting room to try it on. If it's too big or too small, you leave it at the store. When you're leading, you want to find the right style to fit the situation. Leading isn't "one size fits all." What we've learned in our work with young leaders is that they typically resort to a single way of leading that seems most natural to them, whether or not it fits the situation. (Actually, we tend to see the same thing with adults as well.) The problem is that no one style is effective in every situation. Therefore, if you're using the same approach over and over, chances are, you're being less effective than you could be. The goal of this chapter is to help you identify the four primary leading styles and consider alternatives to your favorite.

A leader's effectiveness is related to the ability to choose the most productive style, based on the circumstances. "Sitch" leading is short for situational leading, the idea of adapting your leading style to fit a certain situation. The four styles are Tell, Sell, Gel, and Del.

- **Tell:** The leader tells team members what to do, without significant interaction with the team, such as gathering their ideas or feedback.

  Strengths: Tell works well in situations where time is of the essence, the team may be less motivated or confident, or the leader is adequately informed and competent, as long as the leader is clear and communication is direct and to the point. During emergencies or highly urgent matters, Tell is preferred, but for short-term use only.

  Weaknesses: The downside of Tell is that people don't like to be bossed. Therefore, when leaders use this style, they run the risk of offending people on the team, possibly making them less motivated to participate. Plus, leaders don't always select the best ideas. Most Tellers use their ideas, limiting input from others.

• **Sell:** The leader asks a few team members for ideas, selects the best one, and then "sells" it to the team.

Strengths: Sell increases the support from team members who get to participate more than in Tell situations, improving the chances of using the best ideas, since more than one are discussed. The approach is still relatively efficient, though a bit longer than Tell.

Weaknesses: Leaders who choose Sell, but don't use others' ideas can be seen as insincere and manipulative—"You ask for our ideas, but never use them." Also, the best ideas still may not emerge because of the limited time. When a majority doesn't participate, there is less ownership by the team and weaker commitment as a result.

• **Gel:** The leader engages the team to participate and discuss ideas, and then moves the team toward consensus. The leader helps the team "gel" toward a common strategy, getting things together. (For our international friends, the word is slang for gelatin, a watery substance that solidifies into a rubbery form. A gelatin food brand is Jell-O.)

Strengths: Gel increases the likelihood that good ideas will emerge and be more thoroughly inspected. Team consensus improves. Members become owners of the process—not just renters—elevating commitment. Potentially weak solutions are identified and hopefully avoided.

Weaknesses: Gel takes a lot of time and can waste team effort by discussing nonproductive ideas. Taking too much time can result in lost opportunities. Another risk is that influential team members promoting their own agendas can hijack ideas. Keeping Gel going in a healthy, productive manner takes good people and meeting management skills.

- **Del:** A leader may choose to *dele*gate, transferring authority and sharing responsibility. Ultimate responsibility still resides with the leader. Using Del to avoid leading and dump responsibility shouldn't be confused with true delegating. Expanding a leader's influence through others and developing them is the essence of Del.

Strengths: Del is a more sophisticated leadership style that empowers others to develop themselves and share power, authority and the rewards.

Weaknesses: Be careful not to overuse Del in young-leader development, because it can become a way to avoid responsibility or difficult work, creating a way to blame others, and producing holes when accountability is lacking.

Here are four brief situations where a certain style of leadership is most appropriate. Read these and see if you can determine which style fits best (answers at end of chapter):

1. You have to create a skit for a school assembly next week, explaining what your student council does to serve others; and this weekend is a three-day weekend.

2. You're at baseball practice after school and one of your teammates gets hit with a baseball and has a bloody nose. The coach isn't there yet.

3. You're planning a school-wide program for each class to become more ecology minded. You'll be working with clubs, classroom reps, and even the adult staff to implement these ecological policies.

4. You're attending a summer retreat and are leading a session to plan student-council-sponsored events for the coming school year.

Final Suggestion

One of the most important things you can do in a leadership situation is what we call "pushing the pause button." This is taking a moment before you jump into leading, to consider which style best fits the situation. If you don't do this, chances are you'll automatically begin leading from the style you're comfortable with, whether or not it fits the situation best. A good thing to do after observing or participating in a meeting or leadership session is discuss which style the leader used and whether or not it was effective.

Leader Reflections:

1. Which sitch style is your personal preference?

2. Describe a recent situation where you used this style?

3. Describe a situation where your style would not be as effective.

4.   Describe a recent leadership situation (where you weren't the leader) and name the style the leader used.

Answers to situation descriptions:

1. Sell: Time is limited, but you want to create ownership and try to come up with good ideas for your presentation.

2. Tell: There's no time to stand around and talk about what to do. Someone needs to take charge—"Kelsie, get ice. Jill, go call the coach! Who has a phone if we need to call an ambulance?"

3. Del: You've got time and you're going to need a lot of other leaders to pull off this school-wide effort.

4. Gel: You've got time and need to be sure that your council has consensus on what it's going to sponsor, so you can improve the chances of ongoing support.

CHAPTER 9

DESIGNING LEADERSHIP EXPERIENCES

Developing Your Own Personal Growth Strategy

Some of you may be reading this book as part of LeadYoung's LeadWell training program. If so, you know that in addition to small activities within a club session, you're developing a larger leadership project that involves everyone's participation.

Whether or not you're in LeadWell, you'll want to develop your own leadership potential so that you don't have to rely fully on trainers or other adults. This is what great leaders do intuitively—seek opportunities where they can lead. We want to help you do this more intentionally and effectively. This chapter will give you a blueprint for creating your own leadership projects that develop your leadership muscles. Leading is unique. Just as a tennis player, golfer, soccer or football player, gymnast, or runner develops specific muscles based on the specific sport, leaders need to exercise and "lift weights" that will strengthen their social influence abilities.

The reason you want to create your own leadership projects is if you wait for an adult to do it, chances are you won't get a lot of experience as a young leader. Most organizations don't let children, teens, or young adults lead, and even when they do, there aren't nearly enough opportunities as there are young leaders. You're going to have to figure out some of this on your own.

I'm going to introduce you to the primary factors that make up a leadership project. Like a good cookie, if you leave out certain ingredients, it won't be right.

A leadership project contains three primary elements:

1. A clear goal involving change

2. A team of three or more people

3. Authority to make decisions involving risk

Although a leadership project can be far more complicated than these three ingredients, if your project (event, role, or idea) doesn't include these essentials, chances are it won't help you strengthen your leadership muscles.

Clear Goal Involving Change

Setting, pursuing and accomplishing a goal doesn't make you a leader. A non-leader can do that. Simply setting a goal where you're in charge of people continuing what they've been doing doesn't require leading. Leading is about creating change among people. It means that you're taking them a different direction than either they want to go or were originally going. Sometimes, it may not be as much of a change of direction as a change of speed. In other words, you're not just maintaining things. That's what we call managing, keeping things going, pretty much the way they already are.

Managing isn't bad. We have to manage, whether it's paying bills, being sure the staff shows up at the restaurant, or keeping the streets paved. But good managing (maintaining) is generally different than leading. Usually, people good at one are not good at the other, although exceptions exist. Therefore, if you want to create a leadership project so you can practice your leading, be sure the goal involves some kind of change. Perhaps it's starting something from scratch, whether a new club at your school or a fund-raiser, or even resurrecting a program that is dormant or has been stuck for a long time. These require change.

A law of physics says, "A body in motion tends to remain in motion, and a body at rest tends to remain at rest." So when you're setting the goal, does it involve a real change or is it more of the same?

Team of Three or More

A goal involving change isn't necessarily leading if you can do it by yourself or with a friend. The stronger a leader you are, generally, the more people get involved in the project. A minimum is three. Every time you add another person, you make the task of getting them to work together more difficult. Obviously, it's not just a numbers game. The strongest leaders get other leaders and participants to work together, whereas those who only get followers to follow them are not as strong. Getting people with differing opinions together to accomplish something as a team is not easy.

Doing a project alone or with a friend is different than with two or more other people. Maybe they're siblings or a few friends. Perhaps they're fellow students in your school or on your athletic team. It could even be a community-wide program that gets strangers to work together. I know teens who've created organizations involving people around the world to give to a worthy cause, helping people in need.

These projects require different types of leadership. They're opportunities to exercise leadership skills. When you do things without getting others involved, you may be learning responsibility, but not necessarily leading. That's why I'm not a big fan of organizations that require their "leaders" to accomplish projects that can be done alone. Leadership is a social thing. You can't lead by yourself, at least not the way we're defining it in this book.

Three might not be a magic number, but we believe it's the minimum that requires authentic leading. So when you're figuring out what it is you want to do, be sure there's room for others to get involved, requiring you to interact with them and getting them to work together in the task.

Authority to Decide and Take Risks

Here's the kicker for a lot of young leaders. Chances are you're going to have to negotiate with adults who'll want to give you nice, safe little tasks that don't really help you become a leader. In most cultures, teens are treated more like kids in terms of their leadership ability. Parents, teachers, coaches and employers typically try to make it safe for you. So although you'll have to prove yourself a bit, you'll also need to negotiate your ideas to include an element of authority to make your own decisions and take risks. (By risks, we're not talking about physical safety as much as to risk failure of various kinds.)

You can find a lot of projects where adults try to get you to do things for or with them. Maybe it's a community service project such as serving the homeless, cleaning up a dirty lot, or raising money for the organization (e.g., selling candy or discount cards). But most of these projects are about you following, not leading. To truly lead includes an ability to make decisions that involve risk. Giving up control (required to let you make decisions) usually isn't high on a parent's or teacher's priority list. The older you get, the responsibility and opportunity to make risky decisions increases, but leading is about doing this with others toward a goal.

For example, if you're on a student government team, do you have authority to spend budget money (naturally, abiding by certain accountability rules)? Can you decide to spend or not spend a certain amount? What if the project fails; can you make a decision where the outcome could be that you'd lose the money or truly fail? What we want to do is come up with a project that allows you to figure out on your own (or with your team) the best course for you to take. If your parent or an adult sponsor is hovering over you, not allowing you to truly make decisions that you think are best, then you're not really learning how to lead.

Leaders must experience how their decisions are connected to consequences. When you make poor decisions, chances of failing increase. When you make good decisions, chances of success increase. All of this requires risk. Learning to lead isn't about doing everything right. We usually learn more from our failures than our successes. Creating a leadership project must include the chance of failure if it is a good one.

Analysis

When you finish the project, you'll want to reflect and analyze whether or not it truly taught you about leading. You can use the three ingredients to answer seven simple questions:

1. On a 1–5 scale, how would you rate the amount of change required to accomplish your goal?
   1 – None   2 – Very Little   3 – Some   4 – Quite a Bit
   5 – A Lot

2. On a 1–5 scale, how would you rate how clear your goal was?
   1 – Dark   2 – Dim   3 – Clear   4 – Very Clear
   5 – Crystal Clear

3. On a 1–5 scale, how many other people (not counting you) were involved in the project?
   1 – None   2 – One Other   3 – Two to Five Others
   4 – Six to Ten Others   5 – More Than Ten Others

4. On a 1–5 scale, how many people reported directly to you?
   1 – None   2 – One   3 – Two to Five   4 – Six to Ten
   5 – More Than Ten

5. On a 1–5 scale, how much authority did you have to make decisions?
   1 – Little to None   2 – Not Much   3 – Some
   4 – Quite a Bit   5 – A Lot

6. On a 1–5 scale, how much risk was involved?
   1 – Little to None   2 – Not Much   3 – Some
   4 – Quite a Bit   5 – A Lot

7. On a 1–5 scale, how much did this help improve your leadership ability?

   1 – None   2 – Not Much   3 – Some   4 – Quite a Bit
   5 – A Lot

Add the totals of your answers. If the score was 14 or less, chances are, you learned little about leading. If your score was 15-21, leading content was modest. If your score was 22 or more, there's a good chance you learned leading. The next time you do it, how could you increase the total? Better yet, how could you elevate the total before you implement the project?

Project Reflection:

1. What about the project went well?

2. What didn't go well?

3. What are two or three specific things I did well as a leader?

4. How could I improve as a leader (what did I learn from this)?

5. How could I improve this leadership project?

Leader Reflections:

1. What is one idea for a leadership project you could create?

2. What are the three ingredients in terms of your project?

3. What could be done to strengthen it?

4. What would it take to implement the project/get it going?

5. After you do the project, analyze it: What went well, what didn't and why? What would you do differently next time?

CHAPTER 10

FINDING A MENTOR

What's a Mentor?

A mentor is a wise and trusted senior sponsor or advisor. The term originally came from Greek mythology about a character named Mentor, who was a father-like teacher.

A mentor is a person more experienced than you, who can help you learn from his or her experience and thus speed up your development. This person is usually older, but not always. Chances are, as a young leader, you'll be looking for a leadership mentor who is older than you, is a proven leader, and is willing to spend time talking to you about leading, even on a short-term basis.

A mentor is a bit different than a parent, teacher, trainer, coach, counselor, or simply an older person. This person has wisdom that comes from life experience—in this case, leading. A leader mentor may not be formally educated. If the person is humble or has strong natural abilities that she has not reflected on, she may not feel confident talking to someone like you about leading. But nevertheless, people like this can give you a lot of great understanding.

Why Find a Mentor?

People who work in finance understand the concept of OPM (other people's money). OPM lessens a financial advisor's risk as well as allowing her to invest without having a lot of money. The same is true of OPE, other people's experience. Leaders learn through failures and successes, so when you tap into someone else's wisdom, you're potentially avoiding some of your own failures.

Naturally, there are some things you can't learn from another person. That's why in many ways, history repeats itself. You can learn things at 30 that you won't or can't at 20. The same is true of 40, 50, 60 and beyond. But you don't have to learn everything by yourself. A smart young leader will significantly increase her growth by leveraging other people's experience. This gives you a head start over other leaders who don't ask questions or find mentors, and therefore are limited to learning from their own successes and failures.

One of the strengths most teenagers and twenty-somethings have is a thing psychologists refer to as idealism. Typically, in this stage of life, you feel like you can be hugely successful. Many your age also believe that people older than you are often old-fashioned and stuck in a rut. Idealism is good in that it gives you a sense of hope and drive that often gets knocked out of people as they age. This attitude can be bad however, because it can make you think you're smarter than you really are, so you don't ask other people for their ideas or wisdom.

How great would it be if you could literally import wisdom and avoid failures? That's not going to happen. But if you're smart, you'll learn some basic lessons about leadership from your mentor so that when you start leading yourself, you'll be able to recognize situations that your mentor described and then take advantage of this information. Wisdom is power, and power is the commodity that leaders deal in. Tapping an older leader's experience is like driving versus walking, or flying instead of driving. You'll get to your destination faster. You'll grow more quickly as a leader if you harness the wisdom of those who've gone before you.

How to Find a Mentor

The best way to find a leader mentor is to look for these qualities:

1. **A proven track record of leading.** This individual may be a CEO, company president, entrepreneur,

school superintendent, or a community activist. Don't merely look for people in high positions because sometimes, these people aren't strong leaders. Ask adults about leaders they know in your area.

2. **A person near you.** You can think of people in the news from other cities, states or countries, but your best chance to spend time with a mentor is to find someone who's local. An exception might be if your family is vacationing in another area or if you're old enough to travel to meet the person.

3. **A person you may have access to through a contact.** The higher the leaders and greater their influence, the more difficult it'll be to spend time with them. Therefore, it helps to find someone you know who can access the leader. (This is a type of leading up, isn't it?) Perhaps you go to school with the leader's son, or the leader's golf buddy's daughter, or next-door neighbor's kid. Perhaps your parent, a family friend, or a relative knows the leader. Talk to these individuals to see if they will contact the leader on your behalf. It's nearly always better than a "cold call," contacting the leader without any direct connection. These people are bombarded by people requesting their time, so you need to be able to get their attention with more than an e-mail, phone call, or random letter.

For example, let's say that your dad knows the CEO of a large organization with its headquarters near you. If you call this person, you'll end up talking to his secretary, who'll probably say the CEO is too busy to set up a meeting. Therefore, you'll want to let your dad contact the CEO through his contacts. This will increase the likelihood of getting a meeting to at least present your idea. One of the most important things you can do to recruita mentor is to establish clear expectations.

The best way to do this is to suggest a single, short meeting. This will give you the opportunity to not only meet the leader, but also open the door for more opportunities if the leader likes you. This is not your decision, so start simple and make it as easy as possible for the leader to say yes. Many adults think that mentoring involves a big time commitment as well as a special skill set such as teaching, coaching, or counseling. That's not true. Mentoring can be as simple as a leader being shadowed (followed) by a mentee during a meeting, or having a short conversation where you ask the leader some questions.

When the prospective mentor is asked, he may think, "What would I say? What if this student doesn't think much of my leadership after we talk? I have so much going on, it would be much easier just to say 'Sorry, but no thanks.'"

Therefore, your job is to sell yourself and the opportunity of being mentored. Here's a sample letter:

Dear Ms. Clark,

My name is Jesse. I have heard wonderful things about your leadership, and I know that you are a very influential person. I am a 17-year-old student who is studying leadership and involved in a junior executive training program. I would be very honored to meet with you for a few minutes, not more than half an hour. If you do not have time to meet with me personally, I would enjoy sitting through an upcoming lunch or meeting you have, where I can simply observe how you lead and interact with others. I realize that your time is very valuable, and I would not ask this if I did not believe I could learn from you.

If you would like to meet personally, I can even send a few questions that we can discuss, if that would help make our time more productive. Otherwise, I have a short list of questions about leading that I would like to ask. Again, thank you for considering this request. I greatly value your time and expertise investing in a future leader.

Yours truly,

Jesse Nelson

How to Train Your Mentor

This may sound crazy, but most people qualified to be mentors have never been trained on how to mentor. Therefore, most leaders need a little bit of training. Depending on your age, confidence level, and the amount of influence you have with the person you're seeking to be your mentor, you'll have to decide how to go about this.

One thing leaders say when asked to provide a brief mentoring opportunity is, "What do we do? I wouldn't know what to say." If you sense this is the case, you may want to offer a list of ideas. This will hopefully make the yes easier to get. You can rewrite it to make it more like you, but here's an idea that I'm giving you with my name on it, just in case you want to "blame" someone for these ideas, so you don't sound pushy.

Dear Leader:

One of the most important things you can do is invest your time in the life of a young leader. People like you often underestimate the impact you can have as a short-term mentor, and also wonder what to do or say. Giving a few minutes or hours to a young leader is a great way to leave a legacy for the next generation of influencers. Just in case you want something to talk about, here is a starter list you might consider:

1. *Talk to the young leader like an adult, a future leader. Do not worry about "dumbing down" your conversation. Consider how you would talk to a new friend or outsider who may not know about your industry or profession.*

2. *Tell the young leader what you do. Provide a simple explanation of what your company does. Many of us do our work without thinking a lot about it, especially if we have been doing it for a while. Do not worry about trying to impress or entertain the young leader. Be yourself.*

3. *Describe how people in your organization function as teams. How do you interact with them? What are the primary tasks of the teams and team members?*

4. *Show him or her your work environment. This may involve attending meetings, visiting a job site, or taking a look at your office. If needed, introduce the young leader to others. This esteems the young leader. It also models your belief in mentoring and investing in future leaders to your team members and colleagues as they see you interacting with a protégé.*

5. *Think of a problem you faced and how you attempted to solve it. Do not worry about all the details; simply explain a challenge to illustrate what you did. People looking from the outside rarely see the difficulties you face. Consider asking the protégé what he or she might have done in that situation.*

6. *Ask the young leader about his or her goals/ aspirations. By showing interest and asking questions, you're esteeming the young leader. Plus, you are discovering potential areas where their interests and what you do overlap.*

7. *Ask the young leader open-ended questions. Instead of asking, "Did you think the meeting was interesting?" ask, "What was something you thought was interesting during the meeting?"*

If you enjoyed the time, you may offer to do it again. If not, do not worry about extending an invitation, and do not feel badly about it either. Some young leaders will naturally resonate with you, based on their age, personality and interests. Others may not, but that is OK. You've done a good job by simply being available.

Sincerely,

Alan E. Nelson, EdD
Founder of LeadYoung Training Systems

Questions to Ask Mentors
Most leaders are as unfamiliar with being a mentor as young leaders are with being mentored. Therefore, you want to make it as easy on them as possible. Most leaders

will appreciate it if you come prepared with questions. Bring a pad of paper and pen to take notes. Here's a list of possible questions. You may not want to ask the entire list, but select a few that seem to fit the situation.

- What do you do in your work?

- How did you get into your career?

- When did you realize what you wanted to do?

- What do you like about your job? What do you not like?

- Who was influential in your life when you were young, and why?

- What are some goals you are trying to achieve?

- How do you help people work together to accomplish these goals?

- Can you explain a recent example of this?

- How do you try to solve problems?

- What have you learned about leadership over the years?

- How would you describe your leadership style?

- What are your strengths?

- What is one mistake you've made and what did you learn from it?

- What advice would you give me as a young leader?

- As you think about the future, what opportunities do you see for your organization?

- As you think about the future, what problems do you see for your organization?

- What is one thing you would still like to accomplish in life?

- If you could change one thing about your work, what would it be?

- What would you recommend I read?

- What would you recommend I do to improve my leadership?

Wrap-Up

Don't just settle for one or two mentors. Find half a dozen people who might spend time with you, either in person or over the phone, for an interview. Each leader will provide a different perspective. Take notes. Be sure to write a genuine, handwritten thank-you note. Although you're not looking to network or for an open door, realize that if this leader is impressed with you, opportunities may become available for further mentoring or even an internship or job. But if the leader feels used in any way, chances are, the door will close, so seek mentoring opportunities for what they are—a way to learn from someone with a lot of experience.

Leader Reflections:

1. What gets you excited about finding a mentor?

2. Name some potential mentors you may know. What is it you'd like to learn from each one?

3. What would be your strategy for connecting with each one of these?

4. What was most helpful to you in this chapter?

CHAPTER 11

EFFECTIVE FEEDBACK

Giving Good Feedback

Feedback refers to information that provides ideas, responses, and opinions about how well someone or something is doing. For example, you may have been to a restaurant and the waiter or manager has asked you to go online to complete a survey about the quality of their service and food. The goal of feedback is to gather points of view that help the person, organization, or product improve.

Feedback can be very valuable for leaders because it allows them to get information to help the team be more effective, as well as their own leading.

Sadly, far too many adult leaders are really lousy at giving and receiving valuable feedback. One of the most important things you can learn as a leader is how to make sure effective improvement ideas are communicated. Unfortunately, leaders often fail to give positive feedback and they give constructive feedback negatively that intimidates people, because they are rude and insensitive. At the same time, people rarely provide useful feedback to leaders because they fear being punished due to the leader's anger. Obviously, this has more to do with negative feedback than positive, but either way, both are needed when appropriate.

When you as a leader don't provide sufficient feedback to people on your team, you aren't doing your job to help them improve. When you don't make sure the team analyzes how it's functioning, you fail to develop the team. But if you provide feedback in a way that offends people, that's not good either. How many times have you heard someone giving an opinion or making a comment that seemed rude and dishonoring? Probably a lot. When leaders do this, we don't enjoy being around them and usually respect them less.

In our LeadWell training program, we practice giving and receiving peer feedback on a regular basis, along with helping leaders review their own performance after activities. Participants take time to write their ideas about what went well and what could be changed to make these activities better next time. We train them to be specific and brief, and to do it in writing so others can read them.

Three Points for Great Feedback:

1. **Be aware.** Providing quality feedback will be difficult if you're not paying attention to what the team members are doing. Prepare to provide feedback. To do this, you'll need to stay engaged and alert.

2. **Keep the feedback constructive.** Be positive. Find something good to say. Focus on what went well and then what could be done next time to be even more effective. Good feedback is usable information. If you make someone mad by being offensive, that information will not be used.

3. **Try to be specific.** "You did a good job" isn't very helpful. Try to be more exact. "When you asked Ben for his idea, you made him feel included, and I noticed he got more involved at that point. Good job."

Following are a few things to consider when you're observing another person leading. You could write answers to these questions or where appropriate, give a numerical grade from 1 to 5 (1 very low, 2 okay, 3 good, 4 very good, 5 great).

LeadYoung

Team

___ 1. How did the leader communicate with team members?

___ 2. How did the leader do in providing clear directions?

___ 3. How did the leader affirm the team members during the activity?

___ 4. How did the leader handle conflict on the team?

___ 5. How did the leader listen and gather ideas and input from the team?

___ 6. How did the leader help people match task roles with their strengths?

___ 7. How well did the leader stay primarily focused on the team vs. the task?

Task

___ 1. How did the leader help the team strategize toward the goal?

___ 2. How did the leader help the team stay on task?

___ 3. How did the leader keep the team aware of the time and limited resources?

___ 4. How did the leader help the team improve and restrategize?

___ 5. How did the leader assist the team in solving problems?

___ 6. How did the leading provided affect the task's outcome?

___ 7. What was the leader's balance between being task-oriented and people-oriented?

Style/Summary

___ 1. Was the primary style Tell, Sell, Gel, or Del? Did it fit the situation?

___ 2. What else, specifically, could help the leader improve next time?

Receiving Feedback Well

No one enjoys being criticized or critiqued, at least not if you're normal. Yet, receiving continual feedback on how you're doing as a leader will make you better. Therefore, you want to be able to not only give feedback well, you also want to be able to receive it well.

Unfortunately, everyone will not be good at giving you feedback as constructively and positively as you want to do as a leader. In a lot of organizations, leaders are mean. They treat their employees, colleagues and teammates poorly. People excuse ineffective feedback giving with responses such as, "That's just the way it is. You have to have tough skin around here. We all have to pay our dues. That's what it's like being new." That's just ignorant. Receiving constructive feedback need not be painful. Leaders don't have to be insensitive. Leaders who are rude, crude and offensive have never learned how to provide effective feedback, or simply lack the emotional intelligence (EI) about how their negativity affects others.[1]

As young leaders, you'll want to learn how to receive feedback and perspectives from others, even if they aren't very good at giving it. Don't let their inability limit your improvement.

When someone makes a suggestion to you about how you're leading or the decisions you're making, here are some responses you can give as a way to avoid appearing defensive or angry:

- *"OK. Thanks for feeling that you can share that."*

- *"Help me understand how you're feeling."*

- *"I want to improve. What else do you think I can do to be more effective?"*

- *"That's interesting. Let me think about that for a while."*

---

[1] Emotional intelligence (EI) is a person's awareness of how he or she seems to others. It also involves reading other people, their emotional state, and how they're interacting with each other.

- *"Tell me more about how I may be miscommunicating."*

- *"What do you need so I can be more effective?"*

Obviously, the quality of feedback isn't all the same. Some people will provide really good information that may hurt, but will make you a much better leader. Others will say things that they think are true, but should quickly be forgotten because either they're trying to hurt you or they're badly misinformed. Still, it's important to listen because most people simply want to be heard. They respect a leader who is willing to listen to them without becoming defensive or seeking revenge.

Self-Aware Leaders

In addition to receiving feedback from others, good leaders are willing to reflect on their own leading. In our LeadWell training program, we teach young leaders how to analyze their leading, so that in addition to receiving feedback from others, they can continually improve on their own.

Here are a few things to consider as you think about your leading. After an activity or meeting, you may want to review this list and even mark three to four strengths as well as two to three areas where you can improve. You could write comments to these actions or where appropriate, give a numerical grade from 1 to 5 (1 very low, 2 okay, 3 good, 4 very good, 5 great).

LeadYoung

Team

___ 1. I communicated well with team members.

___ 2. I clarified the task and the directions were clear.

___ 3. I affirmed the team members during and after the activity.

___ 4. I handled conflict well among the team members.

___ 5. I listened, gathered ideas, and effectively used feedback from the team.

___ 6. I helped people find roles that seemed to best match their strengths.

___ 7. I kept my primary attention on the function of the team more than the task.

Task

___ 1. I effectively assisted the team in strategizing toward the goal.

___ 2. I was effective in keeping the team focused on the task.

___ 3. I kept our team aware of the time and other limited resources.

___ 4. I effectively helped the team improve and re-strategize.

___ 5. I assisted the team in solving problems when we seemed to get stuck.

Style/Summary

___ 1. I maintained a good balance between tasks and people.

___ 2. My primary style was Tell, Sell, Gel or Del. (Circle one.) Did it fit the "sitch?"

___ 3. What else, specifically, could I do next time to improve my leading? (Write.)

Affirmations

We want to end Section 1 on a positive note. This idea may be one of the most important things you learn from this book. Perhaps the most overlooked leadership quality is giving regular, authentic affirmations. Throughout my life as a leader and student of leadership behavior, I'm amazed how many people say, "My leader never affirms me," "Our leader never tells us we do a good job," or "The leader in our company is always so demanding and rarely ever thanks us for all our hard work."

If you want to stand out as a leader, make sure you let the people on your team know how much you appreciate them, and frequently use phrases such as "Thank you," "You did a great job," "We appreciate you being on the team," "We couldn't do it without your hard work and commitment," and "We're so fortunate to have you." People will be dedicated to leaders who express their gratitude for followers who show good effort.

Forget about finding perfect team members. You'll never find them, just as you'll never be a perfect leader. Don't use responses such as, "They're paid; they should do a good job," or "No one ever affirms me" as excuses for not letting people know how much you appreciate them. Leaders who give affirmations will receive them. That's one of the laws of the universe—whatever you give, you'll receive.

Your job as a leader is to encourage your team. Let each person know how important he or she is to the outcome and success of everyone else. Smile. Pat people on the back. Write thank-you notes. Send affirming e-mails. Remember people's birthdays and special dates. All of these are examples of how you can let people know they're special. We'll talk more about this in the chapter about honor, but in the meantime, be sure to include plenty of the positive feedback known as affirmation.

Leader Reflections:

1. What are examples of feedback in your life (i.e., grades, coach's remarks)?

2. Why do you think feedback from a leader is so important?

3. Why do you think feedback on your leading is so important?

4. What makes giving and receiving feedback difficult?

ABOUT SECTIONS 2 & 3

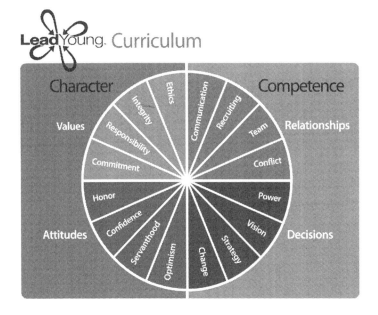

The remainder of this book describes 16 of the most important leadership qualities. I've been studying leadership for a long time. I've seen the professional and personal lives of many leaders. I can't tell you how many coffee shop conversations I've had with leaders, struggling with their marriage, kids, addictions, and ethical decisions that ultimately impacted how they lead professionally. I've had lunches with multibillion-dollar company CEOs/owners; presidential candidates; and a large range of political, corporate, military, and non-profit leaders. That's in addition to the 700 books in my personal library on the topic of leadership, as well as reviewing dozens of leadership trait assessments.

All of this bragging is to lay a foundation for what I'm about to tell you. Of all the leadership qualities I can think of, these 16 are the most important. That's why I picked them for you, to get you going on the right track. They're not the only qualities that make up good leaders and effective leading, but they're the most important. You can find them at the root of more than 90 percent of leadership successes and failures. Because our goal is to help you develop a foundation for a life of leading, we want to be sure it's solid. We refer to these as the "Sweet 16."

What you'll find in looking at these 16 qualities is that about half of them seem to reflect more character content. They tend to be about who you are more than what you know or what you do. People used to say, "Who you are in your personal life doesn't matter in your leading." That's not true. Leaders who lack integrity in one area of their lives are less trustworthy in other parts as well. Leadership suffers as a result. If you ask the investors of companies that have gone bankrupt due to unethical leadership decisions, causing them to lose their life savings, they'd tell you that leader character counts.

Obviously, we'd like everyone to have good character and behave ethically, but it's far more important that leaders have strong character because their decisions impact so many and they have to handle power, a thing that tempts us to behave selfishly.

The other half of these 16 qualities is skills or competencies. They're the things leaders do. These actions separate our leading from others and they distinguish us from those who don't know how to lead.

You'll discover that each of these 16 qualities involves both attitudes and actions. They reflect how we think and how we behave. Each chapter is short, designed to introduce the quality and then give you a chance to reflect on it. One of the goals is for you to apply it. Self-aware leaders are good leaders. They're safe. Leaders who lack self-awareness tend to cause a lot of problems. They have huge blind spots where they tend to fail. How cool it is for you to discover these concepts as young leaders, so you can get a head start on great leading.

Each of the two following sections contains eight chapters, one for each trait or skill represented in the previous graphic. When you get these qualities in your life as a young leader, you'll become the kind of leader that people like me enjoy following.

> THE ONLY REAL TRAINING
> FOR LEADERSHIP IS
> LEADERSHIP.
>
> —Anthony Jay

SECTION 2

CHARACTER

Character: Values

Character represents who a leader is when no one is looking. It's different than reputation. A reputation is what other people think of you. Character and reputation often go together, but sometimes a person who lacks character has a positive reputation because people don't know what the person is really like.

Character represents your value system, the standards by which you live, and the principles you believe are important. It holds the DNA of your behavior, determining how you respond to people, opportunities and temptations. It's important for everyone, but extremely important for leaders because of their multiplication effect: When a leader makes a decision, the results of that decision influence more people than a follower making the same decision.

Character influences how leaders make decisions. It influences how they perceive and treat others. That's why you need to be concerned about a leader's character.

Character represents inner priorities that drive a leader. This internal motivation is an integral part of what makes him or her successful.

There are four primary values that affect a leader's character. They are ethics, integrity, responsibility and commitment. Even though these overlap with other areas of leading, we see them primarily as values. When one or more of these four are flawed or missing, it messes up leading. Therefore, it's important that we understand them and work on making them strong in our lives as leaders.

Character: Attitudes

There are four character qualities best described as attitudes. An attitude is a way of looking at things that affects how we respond to them. How we view something results in how we feel and think about it. For example, if you get a B on a difficult test you thought you might have failed, you're excited. But if you get a C on a test you thought you aced, you're depressed. What was the difference? Your response was determined by your attitude, what you thought you'd get.

Leaders who are successful express four common attitudes. Those who are unsuccessful can frequently discover their failure in one or more of these ways of thinking.

Honor, confidence, servanthood and optimism may seem like good qualities for people in general, but they're essential for great leading. These, perhaps more than any of the other qualities, are what cause people to love your leading or hate it. You'll see why people follow those who express these attitudes.

Someone said, "An attitude is contagious. Is yours worth catching?" The attitude of a leader is far more contagious than others. The difference between a thermostat and a thermometer is that a thermostat sets the temperature, but a thermometer reads it. Leaders are thermostats. Their attitude sets the temperature for the team. When a group is doing poorly and reflecting a negative attitude, the first place to look is at the leader's attitude.

The last four chapters of this section highlight four of the most pivotal attitudes that leaders express in terms of how they impact the leadership process. As you improve your attitude in these areas, you'll increase the results of your leading.

CHAPTER 12

ETHICS

Ethics in Leading

Ethics has to do with the standards by which leaders conduct themselves. This has to do with the way they treat people, respond to laws, and strive to do what is right and fair. Leaders' personal ethics provide motivation to what they will do with others. In the old days, people thought that how leaders lived personally had little to do with what they did in public. But now we realize, after scores of scandals and corporate problems, it's difficult to separate the two. A person who cheats on the golf course is likely to do so in the boardroom. A leader who tells "white lies" to family will also lie to business associates.

Leaders who lack high ethical standards are prone to cut corners, think of themselves over others, and eventually undermine the organization they are responsible for serving. Leaders, by nature, tend to be risk takers. They create change and strive to improve things, so we're not talking about playing it safe by not doing things differently, not pushing back on standards that seem unfair, or being satisfied with the status quo. But when the risk taking goes too far and laws are broken and people are undermined, leaders hurt the people and organizations they're serving.

Some say ethics are the same as morality. Although there's a connection, ethics tend to be more about social norms and how we treat people and express our values externally. Morality, in general, has more to do with personal ethics, values, and even a spiritual and/or religious dimension. Either way, it has to do with values that guide a person in making decisions. When the person making the decisions is a leader, the results affect others.

For example, let's say you're on a student council at your school. You've been given a budget of $230 for expenses for an event. Part of the event involves a party for your council. You want to have refreshments there,, so you buy $20 worth of soft drinks. On the day of the event, you forget to bring them, but instead of returning the drinks to the store and giving back the money, you keep them for yourself. You justify your action as just one of those things that happens when you're putting together a program like this—no big deal. Then you decide to take the executive team (the three of you planning the event) out to lunch to celebrate the event. It costs $50.

Although we don't have all the details or context of the event, spending $70 of $230, nearly 30 percent of the budget, on seemingly self-centered expenses would seem questionable. That money could've been saved or used more effectively for the event. A leader's ethical standards—many of which are not written or clear-cut—influence the decisions he or she makes.

When businesspeople spend lots of their company's money on entertaining guests, putting on lavish events, and doing deals that go around legal boundaries, it reflects low ethical standards. Taking advantage of an organization and considering yourself justified in doing so because of your low pay or lack of respect from a superior are frequent excuses of leaders who lack high ethical standards. When leaders choose to lead this way, they weaken their influence. Although they may be successful in the short term, they're not in the long term.

Another concern about leadership ethics is that what begins as a small infraction of rules or laws often grows in intensity. A small lie about a deal made with a customer grows when people begin questioning the decision. The leader lies more in order to cover up the previous lie and make it sound like he was being honest and ethical.

Leading is difficult because frequently it's not black and white. Leaders have to make decisions in what we call the "gray area," situations that aren't clearly right or wrong. In the US, we refer to strong ethics as "taking the high road." This means doing what is right, even when it isn't convenient or easy. It also means establishing your standards before you get into situations where people and circumstances would tempt you to lie, steal, cheat, or break the law.

When you're willing to compromise to win at all costs, you'll be a dangerous leader people won't want to follow because you'll be destined to fail. Every week, political, religious, and business leaders are written up in news headlines, fired from jobs, and even imprisoned, because they thought they were above the law and were willing to make unethical decisions. Ethics and character go hand in hand. They can't be separated. When you're a leader with character, you'll have good ethics and make ethical decisions. When you lack character, you'll compromise on your ethics and make decisions based on peer pressure or what will give you the quick win, and do what is likely to create bigger problems for your team and organization. Much of this has to do with how we're raised as kids and even our spiritual beliefs.

Leader-Follower Selection

Another reason you want to be an ethical leader is because people watch what you do and tend to follow how you do things. When you lie, cheat, put others down behind their backs, and push the rules, your followers will do the same. It doesn't work for you to be unethical while hoping your team will be ethical. If you want ethical behavior from your followers, model it yourself.

A difficult situation you'll probably find yourself in as a young leader is when the person above you is making an unethical decision. Do you support it, allow it, quit, or tell someone else about it? There are now laws in the US supporting people who "blow the whistle" on leaders doing unethical things. But this doesn't make it easy.

You'll likely meet some leaders who are really good at what they do, but make questionable ethical decisions. At the same time, you may know people who are very ethical, but aren't as good at leading. We'd all like to follow leaders who are both good and ethical, but it doesn't always work that way. My suggestion is when you find yourself in a situation like that, choose the more ethical leader. Although the organization may not be as effective short term, the unethical leader will eventually do things that both hurt herself and the organization she's supposed to help. If you're associated with this unethical leader, it may go against you as well.

Similarly, when you're leading and people on your team are making unethical decisions, you need to take a stand. Either confront the rule breakers or relace those members with more ethical ones. The role of the leader is to establish a high ethical standard by which others operate.

Some people say that ethical leading isn't difficult— just stick to your standards. That's not true. Leading ethically is difficult because there are so many variations of what is and isn't wrong based on differing opinions, situations, and pressure to win or not. But when leaders make poor ethical choices, people will pay for it. They may get away with it for a while, but eventually, unethical leadership nearly always catches up to you, and not in a good way. History is scarred by unethical leading. The future will be bright if you lead ethically.

Leader Reflections:

1. Describe an ethical leadership situation you've experienced as a leader or follower.

2. When has a leader you've known disappointed you in an ethical area?

3. Name some values you believe are important as a leader.

CHAPTER 13

INTEGRITY

What You Say Is What You Do

By now, you've probably experienced a number of instances when a friend, sibling, parent, or even a teacher or neighbor, disappointed you because they didn't keep their word. They said one thing and then did something else. No one's perfect; sometimes we don't keep our word or we fail to follow through. But when this becomes common, you have a problem. People won't trust you anymore. They won't believe what you tell them. This is an example of lacking integrity.

When a leader lacks integrity, it's a bigger problem because it involves other people. Leaders get us to do things we normally wouldn't. They help us give up time, energy, money and talent to work on a project together. They get us to give of ourselves toward a common goal. Leaders have to create trust so that people will follow them and want to be on their team. A lack of integrity results in a lack of trust. A lack of trust results in people not following a leader. People need to trust leaders before they're willing to follow them. When trust is not there, people don't participate, or at least not to the level they need to or could.

The word integrity means "whole," "complete," and "one." An "integer" is a whole number, not a fraction or partial number. Having integrity means that you are whole. You're not divided in what you say and do. Similar words for integrity are honesty, truth, honor, reliability and uprightness.

Although we want our friends and team members to have integrity, it's very important that we have this as leaders. When a leader deceives his team, when he says he'll do one thing and either doesn't follow through or does the opposite, people get hurt.

Let's say that Amanda was the president of her club at school. She wanted to get more people into the club, so she talked the other club members into committing to a party so they could invite their friends to come, have fun, and then learn about the club, in hopes they might join. Amanda said she'd talk to the principal to reserve a room for the party. Weeks came and went and Amanda kept making excuses. First she said she forgot, then the principal was out of town, and then she sort of told a fib, saying that the secretary was supposed to get back to her about a date but didn't. Her team members were doing their part, but when they didn't have a location two weeks from the event, the members decided to postpone it. "We can't have everyone come to a party when we don't even have a room," they said. When Amanda wasn't around, some of them would say to each other, "Amanda keeps making excuses. She's not doing what she said she'd do. We need to get another club president."

People will test you as a leader before they follow you with all of their heart. They're going to be watching you, how you treat people, and if you keep your word. They'll be watching for gaps between what you say and what you do. The more frequent and larger the gaps, the less they'll be willing to trust you because this is a lack of integrity. You're not "whole"—you're undependable.

Types of Integrity

There are various ways that a lack of integrity is expressed, many of which affect a leader's ability to get people to follow and work together:

- **Saying one thing and doing another.** We've talked about this. People want to follow leaders who'll do what they say they'll do. Whether it's keeping an appointment or accomplishing a task, people will be less committed when the leader is unreliable.

- **Not following through on responsibilities.** You want your team members to do what they commit to and what you ask them to do. When you don't follow through with a task, you're communicating to them that this isn't an important value. This erodes a team's ability to depend on each other, thus affecting the results. (We'll talk more about responsibility in the next chapter.)

- **Talking negatively about people who aren't present.** One problem of modeling this as a leader is that your team members will begin thinking that you approve of them doing the same thing. They'll start saying things about you if you offend them. They'll talk about teammates in ways that keep the team from being united.

- **Establishing standards and acting like they don't apply to you.** Leaders have to set expectations for the team—"We need everyone to arrive on time," "We need you to be committed to this team," "We don't spend more than our budget." Every organization has values and expectations definedin unwritten and written rules. But when leaders go against these rules in the way they act, team members feel disappointed or angry and won't trust the leader as much.

Integrity and credibility go together. Credibility has a lot to do with reliability. A credit card is what a bank gives to people, believing they will pay the loan that the card provides, whether it's a loan for a meal, a new shirt, or a big vacation. A person with a bad credit rating has a difficult time getting a loan because the bank doesn't think the person can or will pay back the money. Your credibility as a leader is what followers will loan you in commitment. When your rating is high, they'll give you a lot. When it's low, you won't get much. A credible leader does what she says.

Weakening Leading Up and Laterally

You can see how integrity and ethics go together. They're important character issues, meaning they tend to reflect who you are and what you value as a person. Leaders sometimes think they can get away with things. Often they do, at first, so they start cheating, lying, cutting corners, and not following through. As a result, they do even more of this, telling bigger lies, cutting larger corners, and covering their deception. But eventually, these will diminish the way people think about the leaders and then they won't trust them anymore.

Reputation is what people think about you. Character is who you are. Sometimes, a person's reputation is better than his character; sometimes, it's worse. But generally, a person's character will determine his or her reputation. A leader's reputation will often determine whether or not others follow and to what extent. This same reputation will affect what people with more power think about this person (leading up), as well as those with similar power (lateral leaders).

When a leader has a reputation for being untrustworthy, other leaders won't want to work with or even be associated with him. We think we can just move on to another team or organization, but when you disappoint other leaders, their influence can work against you. When there's significant difference between what a leader says and does, or what an organization values and what the leader does, integrity will be questioned. Leaders who lack integrity aren't trusted, and trust is an important part of the leadership process. It keeps people committed, unified, and willing to risk and make sacrifices.

Leader Reflections:

1. How are integrity and ethics similar and different?

2. Why do you think leaders keeping their word is so important for people to trust them?

3. Describe a situation where a leader you know lacked integrity.

4. Describe a situation where a leader demonstrated integrity.

CHAPTER 14

RESPONSIBILITY

Dependable

One thing leaders look for in their team members is responsibility. We want people who are dependable, who follow through on their assignments and don't make excuses. We want followers who own the vision, not just rent it. But this quality is even more important for leaders because with influence comes greater responsibility. The word responsibility may best be understood simply as this, "an ability to respond." People who are irresponsible are unable to respond, either by ability or by choice. As a result, they're undependable and therefore not given opportunities as exciting and beneficial as those who lead. Think of people in your family or network of friends who are responsible. These are people who pay you back when they borrow money, who turn in their assignments when they're due, and who you can count on not to lose their keys and ID.

When leaders lack responsibility, people are less likely to follow them because they don't trust them. Trust is essential to the leadership process. For example, let's say you're in charge of your class project. Everyone is counting on you to make sure that you call a meeting, get a room to meet in, and let everyone know when and where the meeting will take place. But you get busy and forget about lining up the meeting until the last minute. Then you assume that you'll be able to find an open room, so you don't schedule it with the school or see what's available. Then you send a few e-mails and text messages, assuming that they all went through to the people you want to have in the meeting.

On the day of the meeting, only about half of the people show up. When they come to the place you suggested, you discover that the room's locked, so you go to another room and another group is using it. Finally, you find an empty room. After the meeting, you discover that some of the people didn't get the e-mail and a few who did came late but couldn't find you because you gave the room number of the one that was locked since you hadn't reserved it. OK, you get the point. If you've ever had an undependable leader like that, you know how frustrating that can be. If you're a leader like that, people won't trust you if you fail to lead responsibly.

Naturally, you can be responsible and not be a leader. Sometimes, people who never take risks and always have their stuff organized and know where it is claim to be more responsible than leaders. In some ways, they are. But the type of responsibility we're talking about as leaders has more to do with carrying the load of a task or project. It's not that little things don't matter, but leaders are primarily concerned about the bigger things. If you're a leader, determining whether or not you use blue or green streamers at the party isn't nearly as important as if the party happens at all.

Let's think of the opposite. When a leader lacks responsibility (is irresponsible), she doesn't seem to care what others think. She may not honor the time and commitment of others, so she's willing to show up late, forget what she promised to do, and let people down. When you're a responsible person, it's difficult working with undependable people. When you're irresponsible, you disappoint people, making them less willing to follow you and commit to your projects.

Young leaders with strong leadership ability often learn about responsibility the hard way. They get people to follow them, only to end up disappointing the team when they don't follow through. Maybe they fail to communicate or don't show up for a meeting. Sometimes the whole team gets into trouble because of the leader's irresponsibility.

Responsibility keeps leaders awake at night. They feel more weight for the success and effectiveness of an organization than anyone. The irresponsible don't carry this burden. They leave it up to others. They don't seem to care. If you find an irresponsible person in a place of influence, run the other way. This person is a disaster waiting to happen.

Self-Motivation

Much of what you do as a leader needs to be self-motivated. The best leaders are not driven by external rewards like money, fame or power. They don't wait for people to call them; they initiate action—"If it's going to be, it's up to me."

Responsibility is an inner voice that says, "I'm going to follow through, not because I'll get in trouble if I don't, but because this needs to be done." That's one of the ways we identify young kids with leadership ability, by observing their personal drive and sense of responsibility.

In addition to personal responsibility, leaders demonstrate a sense of team and organizational responsibility, different from those who are only personally responsible. Their dependability goes beyond themselves, for the sake of others.

Parents, grandparents, teachers, and coaches can help kids learn responsibility. If you've not learned this as a child, it'll hurt your ability to lead well, because being dependable as a leader is an essential for people to feel that they can follow you. If you didn't have someone teach it to you as a child, you'll need to work hard at developing this quality in yourself as a young adult. Follow through on plans and do what you say you'll do. That builds trust.

The ability to respond in a situation has a lot to do with your character, who you are. Confronting someone throwing trash on the ground and returning a lost wallet to its owner are examples of responsibility. Leaders are responders. They take action, correcting wrongs when they see them and leaving an organization better.

Our son, Josh, played competitive tennis in high school. The club we belonged to had indoor courts, but they charged the teens a fee to play on Sunday afternoons. Josh thought it was too expensive. He didn't think it was right to charge so much when they didn't provide any supervision or instruction. Therefore, Josh formed a club of his own and recruited several of the other players. They played on the free, outdoor courts at the nearby high school. The club shut down its program because so many of the players left. Josh had a sense of responsibility to change a situation. He saw the need to help his friends, who it seemed were being taken advantage of by the tennis club. This is an example of leader responsibility.

The ability to respond to situations requiring leadership is the essence of responsibility. Young leaders who are irresponsible will be tagged as undependable and will lose influence. Although we want all people to behave responsibly, leaders need this quality because they're models for others to follow, and their actions affect so many.

Leader Reflections:

1. Describe a leader who was irresponsible and how that made you feel.

2. Describe a time when you were irresponsible. (Go on, we've all got a few.)

3. Describe a situation where a leader taking responsibility had to do more work than others.

4. Describe a dependable leader you know or know about. What makes this leader responsible in your mind?

CHAPTER 15

COMMITMENT

Self-Sacrifice

Someone is selling you on a brand of clothing she wants you to buy, telling you it's great looking, doesn't cost a lot of money, and is fashionable. Suddenly, you realize that she doesn't wear the brand. You ask, "If you think it's so great, why don't you buy it?"

That's a good question. We're always doubtful of people who don't buy what they're selling. Leaders are in sales. They're selling people on their ideas and goals. They want them to buy into a project, which costs team members energy and perhaps even money. When a leader lacks commitment to a goal, others won't follow, or at least not with much commitment themselves. Commitment causes us to persevere when the task becomes difficult and lacks fun, but it's what separates great leaders from wannabe leaders.

Commitment to a task or goal comes in three levels and sometimes in the following order:

1. **The leader verbally dedicates himself or herself to a task or vision.** This is valuable only if the leader has integrity. A vision statement like, "We can win the championship this season if we work hard. How many of you believe that?" motivates others to do more. The words of a leader are important, because they establish a sense of faith in others.

2. **The leader demonstrates commitment.** It's tough to tell everyone else to get in shape when you're flabby, sitting on the side of the gym. Leaders demonstrate with their actions, if they believe what they say. In most companies, the leader is the one who arrives early, stays late, and works extra hours if needed. If you arrive late, leave early, and take long lunches and vacations, your team isn't going to go out of its way to work hard, because you haven't demonstrated commitment.

3. **The leader is willing to sacrifice.** Periodically, there are times when the vision is so big and the goal so difficult that a leader must lead the way in sacrifice if he's going to effectively draw the commitment of others. Throughout history, many of the great social movements resulted in the visionary dying for the sake of the movement, but that personal sacrifice inspired many others to follow. While every task or goal may not require a sacrifice, leaders are the ones who need to initiate it if they're to raise the commitment level of their team.

Someone said, "If you catch on fire, people will come watch you burn." A leader's passion is a very contagious thing. When you get excited about whatever it is you're doing, you'll find people who want to be a part of it. Commitment is the willingness to attempt great tasks. The US president John F. Kennedy announced many years ago that the US was going to attempt to land a man on the moon, not because it was easy, but because it was difficult. Statements of commitment like that inspire others to follow.

Persevering through the Dip

Persevering is such an important part of leading. Nearly any project that you'll undertake with a team, as a leader, is going to have a "dip." A dip is when you don't seem to be making progress, the resources aren't coming through, the team isn't uniting, or defeat looks inevitable. Throughout history, all leaders have faced difficult times. For Moses, it was getting his people out of slavery. Before the new land, they experienced the wilderness. For Nehemiah it involved rebuilding city walls with the daily threat of enemies attacking his team.

The dip is the portion of the journey when people begin feeling discouraged. Some give up. The problem is that while your team members and followers feel this way, you might too. Wrestling with your own emotions makes leading difficult, especially since you need to be encouraging others.

Every leader experiences this inner battle. Because they often keep this to themselves, we don't hear much about it. This is another example of EI (emotional intelligence). Effective leaders are emotionally intelligent, especially when it comes to going through the dip, because that's when people are likely to feel anger, conflict, disappointment and other negative emotions. Teams often divide at this point. Leaders feel the stress of potential defeat and must fight their own desire to give up. Yet, they must not give in to their negative emotions.

Commitment involves pushing through the dip, persevering past the difficult challenges that any great endeavor or worthwhile cause creates. Sometimes you have to give up because investing more time and energy into a project may be the wrong thing. Admitting defeat isn't easy. When leaders let their egos drive them because they don't want to admit defeat, they also drive their teams to the brink of disaster. During wars, military leaders have unnecessarily caused their soldiers to die when they should have retreated. But deciding when to retreat, when to advance, and when to stand firm creates a strange loneliness that sometimes only leaders experience.

In general, people quit difficult tasks too soon. Leaders must be different. Failing to push through difficult times results in teams losing. As a leader, learn as much as you can about the dip. Ask other leaders. Most won't tell you about it unless you ask. These are the uncomfortable, lonely times of leading, but they're common. Know they'll happen. Commitment to the cause and the team helps you persevere through the dip, and when you do, your team experiences a new level of fulfillment and joy when the victory comes.

Let's say your club is organizing a big promotion to get other students to donate food for the needy in your community. But you keep running into barriers. The principal says they already help poor families by providing cheap meals at school. Your teachers say they don't have time to make an announcement about the program and don't want food boxes cluttering their rooms. Soon your club members start feeling discouraged.

"What's the use?" someone asks. "No one's interested in helping the poor inour school."

"Yeah," another chimes. "Let's do something else."

At this point, you can either agree with them or you can express your commitment.

"I don't care what the adults are saying," you declare. "I'm personally committed to bringing in 500 pounds of food, and if we need to set up boxes outside the parking lot fences in the mornings, we will. Who's with me on this?"

These kinds of statements can be frightening, but they express your dedication to the cause and inspire others to commit. Leaders must be committed if they expect others to follow them.

Leader Reflections:

1. Describe a leader you know or know about who exudes commitment.

2. Describe a situation when you or someone you know demonstrated a lack of commitment. What were the results?

3. Describe a dip you've experienced in a team project. How did the leader help or not help the team persevere through it?

CHAPTER 16

HONOR

The Secret of People

Leaders are in the people business. That's why they need to understand the secret of people. Every person you'll ever meet has an invisible question they're asking you, "Do you value me?" When you fail to answer that question, you'll have a difficult time connecting with them. When they don't perceive that you honor them, they respond with similar dishonor, withholding their resources and even fighting you. The secret of people is this: People want to be honored. They want to be treated with dignity. They want to know that you value them.

Fights, wars, divorce, conflict and many other negatives result when people fail to honor each other. Dishonor takes many forms. It can be cheating, lying, stealing or ignoring. All of these say, "I don't respect you. You don't matter. I dishonor you."

Love is a word similar to honor, but tends to be loaded with a lot of emotions. We say that we love coffee, pizza, ice cream, Facebook, our pet, clothes, and television shows. Love between a guy and girl can involve a heavy dose of feelings and sexual tension. Honor is more fundamental. You can honor people you don't even know or like. You can respond to your enemies with dignity, and as a result, often avoid them working against you.

At the core of all relationships is the underlying value of honor. Several religions have what is commonly referred to as the Golden Rule: Do to others as you'd have them do to you. If you want to be honored, honor others. If you want to be treated with respect, respect people. When we fail to do this, we run the risk of offending people and weakening our relationships.

So what does this have to do with honor? Everything. Leadership is about relationships, people working together toward a common goal. Leaders are social architects. They build bridges between people, who in turn use their talents and resources together. When a leader fails to honor people, this weakens relationships.

The leader's attitude of honor is a major factor in whether or not people follow him.

Understanding the Main Cause of Dishonoring Actions

Great leaders are people smart. That means understanding why people act the way they do. When it comes to dishonoring actions, leaders need to know why people respond as they do to each other. Most of the time, when one person dishonors another, it's because the dishonoring person doesn't honor himself. Valuing oneself is the foundation for giving value to others. You can't give what you don't have. Self-value is another word for self-esteem. When we lack self-esteem, it's difficult to value others adequately.

There are many reasons why people lack self-esteem. Quite often it goes back to early childhood, when parents, siblings and other influencers fail to love and accept us. Some people grow out of this; most don't. The result is a lot of people who suffer from low inner love. People with low self-value tend to think others are treating them the way they see themselves. To preserve the limited value they have for themselves, they strike out at others. They dishonor them, reflecting how they're thinking about themselves.

When leaders understand the connection between a person's dishonoring actions and her inability to value herself, they can respond to the root of the dishonoring actions. What the dishonoring person needs is honor. Thus, confronting a dishonoring person should be done in an honoring way, even if the person is being held responsible for the way she's treating others. When a dishonoring person is on the leader's team, the leader can help that person learn how to honor herself as well as others. When a dishonoring person isn't on the team, the leader should defend the team members. This is the root of many team conflicts. Wise leaders understand when they need to deal with problems, and when they need to deal with the deeper roots of these problems.

Why Is Honor a Character Attitude?

The leader quality of honor would seem to fall in the Competence-Relationships section of LeadYoung's curriculum chart. After all, it's about people. The reason I placed this in the Character-Attitude section is because honoring others is primarily a matter of character (who we are) and attitude (viewpoint, perspective).

People of character realize that all humans are valuable, regardless of religion, personality, values or lifestyle. When we honor them, we are recognizing that inner worth. That's an attitude, a way of perceiving people. How you treat people is an expression of who you are, your character.

People lacking character may have great people skills, based on "what you do for me" or "how you treat me at the moment." Relationships that aren't character-based tend to be temporary and shallow and end easily. People with strong character look beyond the appearance, values and behaviors of others. They see a core value in others and respond to it with honor.

When leaders treat people with honor, they have more committed followers than those who don't. Throughout history, there have been leaders who dishonored their followers, leading by fear instead of mutual respect. But these leaders eventually imploded. Many were assassinated. Some seemed to succeed for a while, but the companies and countries they built were flawed.

Let's say you're walking down the hall at school, on your way to your next class. As you pass a locker, you notice a couple of students standing around another student, intimidating him. As a leader on your campus, you're responsible for influencing the culture of your school. Do you ignore the bullying by walking by, pretending that you don't notice and have something more important to do, or do you stop and intervene? How you respond to this situation is a matter of character. You run the risk of being labeled uncool if you stick up for the weaker student. You probably wouldn't lose much if you didn't say anything. But what should you do? What's the right response?

The problem of bullying is primarily one of dishonoring. A bully verbally and physically intimidates others, usually weaker people. When leaders stand up to this behavior, they run the risk of being targeted by the bully. If the bully is a leader, the other leader may experience the negative influence of the bully's team. Naturally, you have to estimate the risk involved in your decision to confront the bully. Maybe you do it with other leaders, or your team members, or someone else in authority. But communicating honor could be as simple as stopping by the students and asking, "What's going on?" You might ask the bullying students, "Is there anything you guys need?" You may focus your actions on the student getting picked on, "Hey, Joe, how are you doing? Sorry to interrupt; I wanted to talk to you about something."

As leaders we want to honor people on our team and those who aren't. We set expectations for others in how we honor friends and enemies. For example, when a teammate says, "Such and such group is a bunch of morons," you might say, "We're really fortunate to have our team, aren't we?" By moving the attention onto something positive, you model an honoring attitude by not participating in other's dishonoring comments. If you dishonor others behind their backs, chances are, people will dishonor you when you're not around. As a leader, you're a guardian of how people relate to each other. When you allow people to dishonor each other, you allow them to ruin the quality of their relationships. People desire to be honored. Countless leaders have fallen because they failed to focus on this primary need among humans.

Leader Reflections:

1. Why is honor so important for leaders, not just people in general?

2. Brainstorm ways that you can honor someone, even in conflict or when you need to confront

them. If you're studying this as a team, role-play the situation.

3. Describe a time when a leader failed to honor you and/or someone you know. What happened? What could the leader have done that would have made it honoring?

4. Write an honoring note to two people you know.

CHAPTER 17

CONFIDENCE

Facing Fear as a Team

Commitment is the attitude of persevering through tough times. "Hold on. We can do it." Confidence is similar, but provides the added motivation to be bold, courageous and strong. A leader's confidence overflows to others, so they feel confident and want to stick with the team and the task.

Everyone has moments in their life when they feel overwhelmed by fear. One of the things I do is teach leaders how to communicate more effectively. Did you know that the number-one fear people have is public speaking? That's right. People are afraid of standing in front of a group and giving a speech, primarily because it puts them in a position of being judged, criticized and rejected. But that's primarily what leaders do, fill roles where they're potentially going to be judged, criticized and rejected. That's why confidence is vital to leading well.

Fear is a limiting emotion. It keeps us from pursuing our dreams and fighting for what we believe is important. It paralyzes us. That's why confidence is so important as a leader. The ability to demonstrate confidence when people, circumstances, or our own emotions push back against our forward movement inspires others to keep moving forward. When a leader lacks confidence, the team will be fearful. When this happens, the team can't function effectively because fear shakes us.

Confidence isn't easy to talk about to young leaders because two categories of young leaders exist. One is the overconfident. The other is the under-confident. Too confident leaders overestimate their ability and underestimate how difficult it is to lead. During our late teens and twenties, most people are ideological. They think they can do amazing things and will be successful, whatever they attempt. They see the problems older people have caused and believe they can do better. This is common. To a certain degree, it's healthy. This is what propels us forward. But when we're overly confident, we risk leading our team into disaster because we lack experience.

> A young leader once asked his mentor, who was a successful banker, "How did you become so successful?"
> "Good decisions," the banker replied.
> "How did you make such good decisions?" the young leader asked.
> "Wisdom," the banker replied.
> "Well, how did you get wisdom?" the young leader asked.
> "By making bad decisions," the banker answered.

There's a certain kind of wisdom that only comes with time, having led in various situations, and discovery through trial and error. When overconfident young leaders don't realize the challenges or potential pitfalls, they can be dangerous.

The other type of young leader is the one who lacks confidence unnecessarily. In our work around the world, I've seen how confidence varies from culture to culture. Certain cultures hold back and restrict their young people. This can also happen where a family member shuts down a young leader from using her ability. Sometimes it's a matter of self-image (how you think about yourself) and self-esteem (how you value yourself).

When leaders of any age lack confidence, it's difficult to lead people because no one wants to follow a person who doesn't seem to know where he's going or if they can accomplish the goal. Confidence is a matter of self-image (how you view yourself), personality, and most of all, experience. The more opportunities you have to lead and gain training and feedback, the more confident you'll naturally become. What we see in our preteen training program is that graduates have significantly greater confidence than their peers in leadership situations, because they are familiar with leading. They know what to do. This increases others' willingness to follow them because people seek confident leaders.

Let's think of a sporting event. Kelsie is the captain of her basketball team. The team is down by six points against a very strong opponent with two minutes left in the final game of the conference championship. They haven't beaten this team in five years, and everyone knows how difficult a win would be. They've trailed most of the game. Even though Kelsie has her doubts, it won't do her team any good for her to act like there's no hope.

"OK, ladies," she shouts above the fans cheering in the stands. "We can beat this team. I know what some of you are thinking—we've never defeated them—but we've never had a team like we do now. This is our moment. We were destined for this time. Let's go out there and take it to them." The team responds to Kelsie's confidence and plays the best game of their career.

What if Kelsie hadn't said anything? What if she let her own fears persuade her to be quiet? What if she said, "Wow, these gals are tough. What does it take to beat them? I'm so tired. Let me sit out, Coach; put someone else in for me"? She wouldn't have inspired anyone on the team and they would've lost again.

Modeling Courage

The reason we place this quality in the area of character is because confidence comes from within a leader, expressed as an attitude. Though demonstrated outwardly, the drive to achieve a difficult goal is something that the leaders must believe in themselves. When leaders look beyond their own feelings of doubt, thinking of what is best for the team, they are likely to communicate an attitude of confidence.

Throughout history, leaders who've demonstrated confidence have gained the allegiance of others. People are drawn to those who exude confidence. In the animal kingdom, leaders set the pace for the rest of the herd, pack, flock, etc. Human leaders are those who inspire others to go beyond what's comfortable or even what they believe is possible—"We must do this! We can take this mountain! Who'll follow me?" When the leader is fearful, timid and lacks courage, others become timid.

As we said, courage is the other side of the commitment coin. Nearly every significant project has times when even the leader wants to quit. There will be moments of fear, boredom, conflict, and setback that tempt people to quit. The word discouragement literally means "de-couraged." The courage of a leader raises commitment. Great leaders know how to push through the times when the team feels like giving up. Courage and confidence go together.

People seek leaders who help them believe that accomplishing difficult tasks is possible. Everyone wants hope. Those who create this among others emerge as leaders. When we express a confident attitude, we're more likely to help people have confidence in our ability to lead. This happens the minute you walk into a room, when you greet another person and look him in the eyes (at least in Western cultures). Confidence includes how you carry yourself, stand, speak in front of others, how you respond when others challenge you and when circumstances tempt you to doubt. This quality provides invisible glue that causes people to stick together to accomplish a task that is larger than can be accomplished individually. We want to follow leaders who confidently lead us forward.

Leader Reflections:

1. Describe a situation you can remember where the leader lacked confidence. How did it affect the team or followers?

2. Why do you think it's potentially dangerous to follow a leader who's overconfident?

3. What's one thing you'd like to improve on in this area?

CHAPTER 18

SERVANTHOOD

Serving by Leading

In most cultures, when you think about a leader, you don't automatically think of a servant. The two often seem like opposites. After all, isn't leading about getting others to serve you? By now, you know we don't believe that, but this is the way many think about leadership. People think of the CEO as making a lot of money, having a big office, and getting a lot of people to do the dirty work in the organization. We see national leaders and look at the people who make their food, open the doors for them, and bow to them, giving us the idea that this is what leaders dream of and strive for.

But we'd like to paint a different picture of leadership for you. We'd like you to think of leading as a way to serve people. That's right, we lead to serve. Some people serve by teaching, others by using their gifts of selling, physical labor, or engineering safe buildings and bridges. Leaders serve by helping people use their best gifts together.

Leading is a tool. You can use a wrench to fix your car or hit someone over the head. Although the wrench was made to repair things, it can be used as a weapon. The same is true of leading. You can use it to benefit or hurt people. History is full of leaders who've done the latter. Dictators, military tyrants, and ruthless kings and presidents scarred countries they could have served. How a leader uses his influence has a lot to do with his own motives. That's why we put servanthood in the category of character qualities and attitudes.

If you choose a spiritual approach to life, as I do, chances are, you believe in some sort of supreme design. In this view, leadership can be seen as a creator's gift to humanity, helping people combine their different strengths toward a common purpose. One of the reasons we typically pay leaders more is because their roles are so unique. They help all of us be better, like the conductor of a symphony. But because we may pay these people more doesn't mean they should become selfish and take advantage of others. Leaders who are self-centered ultimately hurt the organizations they're designed to serve.

Humility

Howard Greenleaf wrote, "The servant-leader must first become a servant." Servanthood starts in your heart with an attitude of humility. This is a very difficult thing because power is a highly addictive. It tempts us to misuse it. Leaders have to deal with power. They get things done with their influence. Take away a leader's power and you no longer have much of a leader. But that's what makes servant-leading so difficult. Whenever you're in charge, when people look to you for answers, or when you have more influence than others, it's very tempting to use this influence for your own benefit. This turns leading into something other than serving.

You don't have to be poor as a leader, feel bad if you earn a living or make a lot of money, but your motivation should be one of service first. When leaders forget that without followers there's no such thing as a leader, they start to think they're better and more important than they are. That's when their ability to lead runs the risk of taking advantage of people.

One way to keep a servant's attitude is to be willing to do things that aren't prestigious. Don't always take the nicest office. Don't worry when people don't compliment you. When the team wins, give credit to others. Be willing to say, "I'm sorry," "I was wrong," and "What do you think?" These are all ways to communicate that your leading isn't about you. There will be times when people take advantage of you or consider you weak, but your team members will defend you in those times. People want to follow leaders who aren't self-centered or proud or put others down in the process of leading.

Humility's often confused with timidity, lack of confidence and low self-esteem. The humble person can be assertive, confident and possess high self-esteem. The big difference is the leader's attitude. Humility is about character. People with humility are able to put others first. They're willing to go last at times. They're not self-promoting and egotistical. The humble leader has abilities that proud leaders don't, such as the ability to listen well, learn from mistakes, and, as a result, improve more than the boastful leader. Eventually, people see through proud leaders and feel disgusted by them. People want to follow leaders who aren't always trying to lift up themselves.

Let's say you're leading a team of students to raise money for a charity in your community. In addition to going to school and working a part-time job, you put in a lot of hours organizing a big fund-raiser to create more awareness of this charity. At the end of the event, you celebrate the project and congratulate your team. The director of the charity comes to the celebration to present you with a plaque, because you're the leader. But you realize that everyone made it successful. Instead of saying, "Thank you," you say, "I'm accepting this on behalf of all of our team, because each of you added so much to the event. Steve, you did an amazing job with the publicity. Roberto, you put together the greatest refreshments I've ever seen. Anish, the decorations were terrific. I want to say 'thank you' for your work, all of you." That's the spirit of a servant.

Servanthood is a very important quality. Keeping that attitude while leading is difficult, but the world is looking for people who can do that. We've seen so many leaders who treat other people like their servants. As a servant-leader, you're still leading. You won't be doing some of the things that others are; instead, you use your influence to serve them, to do what they can't or won't do.

For you to keep up this attitude, you'll want to be very intentional. This doesn't come easily to most people. Since a majority of leaders are not servant-like in their attitude, you don't see a lot of good examples in the news or in the media. Quite often, we see just the opposite, leaders who lie, steal and cheat because they're selfish. They break laws and get in trouble, and this makes the news. A servant-leader doesn't feel the need to be in charge. He doesn't force his way. He also stands up for those with less power. A servant leader opposes bullies. So never confuse servanthood with weakness, safety or lack of courage. These are never the qualities of leading and certainly not servant-leading.

Leader Reflections:

1. Who's a person you know who seems to act like both a servant and a leader?

2. Why do you think it's so difficult to be a strong leader and a servant at the same time?

3. What can a leader do to develop more humility?

4. Why do you think servanthood isn't more valued in society?

CHAPTER 19

OPTIMISM

Sell Hope

Napoleon, the famous French military leader said, "Leaders are purveyors of hope." What he meant is that leaders inspire people to believe what's possible. They give people hope by showing them a better future. Leaders encourage others when climbing the hill becomes difficult and tiring. They share their dreams, goals and aspirations. Commitment, confidence and opti-mism are related, yet uniquely different attitudes. Com-mitment reflects our willingness to persevere through dif-ficult times. Confidence represents a leader's courage to face fears. Optimism is about our ability to instill hope and inspire people to follow us toward a goal. A person can be confident and negative, and optimistic but lack confidence.

People like hope. They need hope. It gives them a purpose to live, to anticipate a better tomorrow. A leader uses hope to predict success—"Hey, we can ac-complish this! We will win. We can succeed. It's going to be OK. You're doing a great job. Isn't this fun? Wow, look at the possibilities." These are all positive, optimis-tic statements that cause people to hope more. When people hope less, they give up and don't enjoy being on the team.

Therefore, you can see why it's so important for a leader to be positive. When you're going through dif-ficult things and you begin wondering if you'll succeed, you want someone who makes you feel hopeful. When the leader begins to believe his doubts and becomes pessimistic, negative and fearful, everyone else will tend to become that way as well.

One of the most difficult things about leading is han-dling your own negative emotions so you don't discour-age others. When a team begins thinking it's going to fail, often it does. You don't want to be fake. You don't want to pretend things are good when they're not. But you need to give others hope. If people feel like there's no reason to hope, they won't follow you.

Let's say that your school is shutting down a popular snack bar because the administration believes it costs too much to run, and with budgets shrinking they have to cut unnecessary programs. You're sitting with a group of friends and you begin complaining about the school leaders' decision.

"I can't believe it. They keep shutting down things we like," someone says.

"Yeah, what's the deal about that? They make money on it. If we like it, they don't," another responds.

As you listen, you believe they're probably right. You think, "Yeah, who's going to listen to a bunch of students? We won't be around in a couple more years. Budgets are difficult." If you stated your thoughts, chances are your friends would agree and you'd all assume there was nothing you could do. After all, you're just a group of students. But something inside you makes you think, "I'll bet we could do something. Why don't we stand up for what we think is important? I'm tired of students not being heard."

So even though you have doubts you say, "Let's take it back. Let's challenge them. We can put together a petition, get students to run the snack bar, and maybe keep some of the profits for other student programs getting cut. There's no reason why we can't help them figure out how to keep it operating."

Your friends start getting excited. "Yeah, let's do something. Why not?"

Great causes often begin this way. While the situation looks bleak, dismal and daunting, leaders ignite hope among others.

One of the most discouraging things leaders hear is when people say, "*Everyone* is unhappy. *Everyone* is upset. *Everyone* has concerns." Whenever you hear someone use the word "everyone," realize it's always an exaggeration. What they usually mean is "I and a few friends of mine feel this way." If it's a small team, it may mean two or three. If it's a large organization, it may be a small percentage. Ask the person to clarify who "everyone" is by naming names. If the person resists, think of who this person typically spends time around. Chances are, these are the people with the issues. Unfortunately, negative news spreads faster and easier than positive. Therefore, leaders may need to stand up quickly to naysayers and pessimists, to interrupt the spread of negativity throughout the team.

Think What Can Be, Not What Is

Don't be intimidated when other people describe the temperature of a project, team, organization, circumstances, or their own emotions because as a leader you don't think in terms of what is, but what can be.

Leaders possess the discipline to keep their fears to themselves and find the positive in situations. You may need to investigate possible solutions or what people in the past have done to correct a similar problem. Seek positive people yourself. It's not easy to stay optimistic around pessimistic people, but those who follow you need you to remain hopeful.

Obviously, there come times when even great leaders need to admit when a situation is desperate and loss is inevitable, but even then they leave people with hope—"We did our best," "I was proud to serve with you," or "We can all feel good that we stood up to our opponents." Amazingly, even in defeat, leaders have the ability to leave us with hope. They know that people need hope in their lives and are motivated to follow those who provide it.

Optimism when things are difficult isn't easy. Leaders have to honestly confront difficult situations and state the facts as they are, but they don't leave them as they are. They let the team know that in spite of the facts, they'll fight hard, overcome, and in the worst-case scenario, prove that they gave it their all.

Most of us won't face many life-or-death situations, but whether it's being behind in a soccer game or rallying the troops into battle, leaders need to be optimistic. Anyone can be positive when things are going well, but effective influencers keep hope strong when things aren't going well.

Someone said, "Keep your fears to yourself. Give me your hope." People are prone to express their fears verbally. This is what I call "worthless reality." Yes, it may be true, but saying it does no good. It doesn't change the situation. As a leader, sometimes you'll need to confront those who cause people to lose hope because of what they're saying. Remember, you're in charge of the thermostat as a leader. Don't let others turn down the heat. You may need to have a one-on-one conversation with an influencer who is spreading rumors or gossiping. Perhaps you'll need to ask two or three people to stay after a meeting and ask them if what you heard they said is correct, giving them the benefit of the doubt, but letting them know you're holding them accountable. This can strain relationships a bit, but your biggest responsibility is to the entire team. You can't allow a few negative people to discourage everyone else.

This can be difficult because you need to decide when people are merely complaining and when they're providing valuable feedback that will help the team improve. Leaders are often criticized for shutting down people who share news that isn't positive. After a while people stop sharing valuable information that may not seem positive because the leader is defensive and punishes them. When this happens, leaders miss important input that would help them improve the organization. Then the team and organization suffer.

Leaders need to listen well so they can separate the truth from negative emotions. It's like receiving a badly wrapped gift. Just because you don't like the box, doesn't mean you toss the present. Unwrap the gift. Keep it and throw away the wrapping.

Words often reflect our thoughts. They're powerful. What you say as a leader has more impact than what others say. Leaders get quoted. When your words hint at defeat, discouragement, or fear, people will repeat these. Sometimes they make them even worse than they are. When your talk has hope, optimism and positivity, people will feel inspired and motivated. Here are some examples of how you can rephrase a hopeless comment into a "hopemore" response:

Hopeless: We're not going to win.

Hopemore: What makes you think that? We're going to do our best. That's all I ask.

Hopeless: We don't have any money.

Hopemore: Let's see how we can cut back in other areas and brainstorm ideas to see how we can make it happen.

Hopeless: Everyone's unhappy.

Hopemore: Thanks for sharing that. Tell me who you've talked to so we can see how we can improve the situation.

Hopeless: Everyone's so busy. No one wants to commit.

Hopemore: Well I'm committed, and I think we can find some others like us who'll make this thing a success.

That's what we call reframing. You help people see something from a different angle, a positive one. The more you practice this, the better you'll get at helping people remain hopeful, even in difficult situations, because that's what leaders do, give hope. This one quality can make the difference between success and failure when the situation becomes difficult.

Leader Reflections:

1. Describe a situation when you saw how hope in-spired people to keep going with a task.

2. Why do you think it's so important for leaders to be optimistic?

3. Do you have ideas about how a leader can stay optimistic when he or she feels discouraged?

4. Words are powerful. Describe some "worthless realities" and then change them to be positive.

PEOPLE MAKE HISTORY AND
NOT THE OTHER WAY AROUND.
IN PERIODS WHERE THERE ARE
NO LEADERS, SOCIETY STANDS
STILL. PROGRESS OCCURS
WHEN COURAGEOUS, SKILLFUL
LEADERS SEIZE THE OPPORTU-
NITY TO CHANGE THINGS FOR
THE BETTER.

—Harry S. Truman

SECTION 3

COMPETENCE

The definition of competency is: capability, skill, pro-
ficiency, know-how, expertise. Half of the leader qualities we emphasize involve competencies. These lean

toward skills or abilities. An aptitude for leading allows you to learn leadership skills faster and at a higher level than most people. The exciting thing about competencies is that these are more likely to gain you immediate attention as a leader. Four of the qualities in this section have to do with relationships and the other four have to do with a leader's ability to make decisions.

Relationship Skills

The primary relationship skills have to do with recruiting, team, communication and conflict. Most great leaders possess exceptional skills in these areas. So it makes sense that a majority of leadership failures are directly related to a lack of skills in these areas.

The reason for this is pretty simple. Leading is about people. As a leader, you're not working with a hammer and nails, or a computer and software. Your primary resources are humans who are unique, complex, and can willingly decide to follow you or not. People skills alone won't do it because there are a lot of great "people people" who aren't good leaders. A leader needs the other qualities we're talking about. Yet, leaders fail more in this area than any other.

Relationships are the most difficult part of the leadership process. A leader's job is to help people accomplish together what they couldn't or wouldn't as individuals. The challenge we face is getting busy people to give us their time, energy and talent so we can be a unified team, accomplishing tasks together. As we describe the four qualities of recruiting, team, communication and conflict, I hope you'll think about people in your network you can develop into a team. Don't worry about your national government yet. Focus on your friends and classmates with whom you can do great things together.

Decision Making

The other half of section 3 has to do with a leader's ability to make good decisions. A person in the leader role is continually expected to solve problems. Great leaders don't do this alone. When they do, they make more and bigger mistakes. The power of the leadership process is that you tap the potential of the entire team, not just a few. But even after discussion, thinking and research, someone needs to make the decision. Usually that someone is the leader.

Therefore, how a leader goes about making decisions has a lot to do with the success of the team or organization. In the second half of section 3, we'll discuss four primary areas that deal with the decision-making process. These are power, vision, strategy and change.

We refer to these four as "decision-making competencies" because, for the most part, they have to do with how leaders and those who follow them make choices. Power has to do with a leader's ability to make strong decisions. When you take away power, you have less chance to make an impact with your decisions. Vision has to do with the words and ideas we use that inspire other people to follow us, filling them with hope and excitement. Strategy is about deciding the plan we take to accomplish a goal. And change is the way we decide to respond to things we didn't expect, helping our team adapt to new conditions.

Some say that a person's life is the accumulation of the decisions he or she makes. This is even more true of leaders, whose decisions not only affect themselves, but the people they lead. Plus, they affect what the team or organization does in society. Remember, the 16 leadership qualities we're focusing on are not the only ones, but they're the most important because they affect your success and failure as a leader more than others. All 16 qualities impact decisions, but power, vision, strategy and change relate directly to choices a leader makes. By concentrating on the eight skills in this section, others will see you as a leader.

CHAPTER 20

RECRUITING

The Task of Ask

Leaders build teams. To build a team, you need to recruit, which often involves asking people to participate. Sometimes you inherit a team and sometimes you start from scratch.

Before you go out and get your friends to help you, you'll want to consider what it is you want to accomplish, what tasks are needed, and what talents or resources would be required for the task.

The reason you want to do this is because if you recruit nice people who have little talent or desire to accomplish what you want to achieve, you and the rest will be frustrated. Having really nice people and close friends in roles that don't match their abilities will strain even good relationships. Removing a person from a position they're not strong in isn't always easy. Conflict happens. Feelings get hurt. You'll lose sleep. And the team will lose time and energy.

Let's say you are volunteering at a charitable organization that helps needy kids in the community. You want to start a computer club, so they can learn how to use a computer and learn proper online study skills. To accomplish this idea, you may need people who understand computer networking, a marketing person to help you develop a plan to publicize the project, and someone with great people skills to connect with influencers in the different social groups in the community for funding and donations. Then you realize you need someone who can do graphics work, a technician, workers to hand out flyers, and a person who'll keep records on donations and communication.. Each task can be matched with an interest, skill and personality. If you start without thinking of the tasks needed, you may have the right people, but in the wrong places.

Once you've determined what you want to accomplish and what types of skills or talents you need, you'll have to do what every effective leader throughout history has had to do—ask. The "task of ask" works best when a leader personally challenges an individual to be on her team. Leaders often resist this because, well, we're human and we don't like rejection. To ask someone means you run the risk of him saying no. Fragile egos can't handle rejection. Therefore, you want to do your best to share your vision and motivate people to participate. But if you push too hard, you may irritate them and it'll backfire on you. You need to believe in your cause to risk rejection. Remember, a "no" from asking is better than a "no" answer from not asking.

One idea to get people involved initially is to offer a trial period, just to see if they like it. It's like test-driving a car before buying it—"Help us for one month, and if you don't like it, you can walk away without any guilt." Naturally, being a young leader typically involves asking people to donate their time, since most young leaders don't have much of a budget for hiring people. If you do, it's easier to find people, but you also have to find great talent who can justify their pay. Money or no money, leaders must be able to recruit people who'll be on their team, whether it's a softball team, club, political campaign, fund-raising, or community service event.

Don't try to avoid the big ask by putting an ad in the school newspaper or on a social network website. This usually produces limited results. The best people nearly always come through personal contacts, either yours or those of people you know. Even if you find people from a generic sign-up campaign, you'll need to ask the good ones.

Recruiting Challenges

What do you do when you need to get rid of a team member? We call it "de-cruiting." There are many reasons why you may need to ask a person to step down from a position or role. Here are a few:

- The person has a bad attitude and/or doesn't get along with others.

- The person has been performing poorly; low quality.

- The person has done something unethical and/or disloyal.

- The person is overwhelmed by the responsibility (time, commitment, etc.).

These are the most common, but there may be a combination of these or other factors that require you as leader to change a role or ask the person to leave the team. The only thing more difficult than firing a person is being fired. Even though most of you reading this book will not be in an official role to let someone go, it's part of any organization that needs to grow and stay healthy. Telling someone that he or she is no longer needed on a team or that his or her performance isn't up to the necessary standards can be painful. Good leaders often lose sleep over this because they like the person or at least want to be liked by the person.

"Miranda, we really appreciate all you've done for the team. I think we could use your gifts more in another area for a while." "Jason, as our team has developed, we need to make room for people with different talents and skills." "Beth, it doesn't seem like you're enjoying your role as much as you used to. What else would you like to do on our team?" There are a variety of ways you can go about helping a person find a more productive role, while honoring them. But as a leader, your primary responsibility is the health of the organization. That means from time to time, you'll need to let people know that their services and help are no longer needed by your organization.

Since young leaders often work in teams or organizations that don't pay, you may think, "I can't fire a volunteer." Oh yes you can. In fact, you need to, because if a volunteer isn't doing his or her job, your organization will suffer. If someone isn't showing up to meetings, is causing conflict, or is doing a lousy job, you'll need to have an honest talk and explain this. If you allow mediocre behaviors to go on for long, the team and organization will suffer, and other people will get frustrated that you've not addressed this as a leader. They'll think you don't care, aren't good at leading, or aren't in tune with the team. This will hurt your ability to lead in the future as well.

Another difficulty in recruiting is if you have limited resources, such as a lack of rewards that can attract good talent or little talent (if your organization is very small). The main reason companies don't hire more and better people is they don't have enough money. In your world, the issue may not be money, but is related to rewards. Perhaps people you'd like to attract to your team are busy in other things such as sports, religious activities, family commitments, school events, or work. They may be limited by transportation. Very few organizations have all the resources they want, so leaders need to get used to doing the best with what they have to attract people with talent and energy to benefit the team.

Here are some things you can offer people, when you have limited resources:

- This is an opportunity to advance as our organization grows.

- This experience will look good on your resume and get you a better job.

- You can access people you might not be able to otherwise.

- We have a lot of fun and you'll make some great friends.

- You'll be helping people and gaining community service credits.

One thing we've noticed among a lot of young leaders that hurts recruiting is they tend to do too much themselves. Leaders are doers by nature. They like to see progress and get things done. When the leader is doing too much of the task, he isn't able to help the team work together. The task of the leader is to manage the team. This includes recruiting people to participate. The leader can't settle for being a team member. You can't expect to succeed as a leader if you're doing too much of the work yourself. When you're busy doing the task, you're less able to recruit, thus reducing your team's success. Sometimes in our training curriculum, we do not allow the leader to do activity tasks so they can keep their focus on the team. A good leader has to keep an eye on how the team members are doing, who needs help, who's disengaged, and who's about to leave.

Effective leading means recruiting people before they're needed. You're a talent scout. People come and go, so you want to have a few names ready to contact in case one of your team members gets sick, quits, or leaves for whatever reason. If you're too busy to do this, your team will suffer when members leave. Good leaders are always looking for good people, even when they seem to have enough people.

Recruiting is one of the most difficult parts of leading, but it is also critical because the most important single quality of a team is the quality of its members.

Leader Reflections:

1.   On a 1–5 scale (1 = Terrible, 5 = Great), how good would you say you are at the task of ask?

2. Why is it so important to think about the various roles and tasks required to accomplish the goal before recruiting the team?

3. Describe a situation when the right people were in the wrong roles on the team, and it suffered as a result.

4. What do you think is the most difficult part of recruiting a team?

CHAPTER 21

TEAM

A Need to Belong

In the last chapter we talked about recruiting a team. In this chapter, we'll discuss how to help that team work together. One of the greatest resources a leader can take advantage of is people's desire to belong. We have a strong emotional need to be a part of a family, group, tribe, or community. This sense of being a part of something bigger than ourselves is glue that holds teams together, even when the vision is weak and leadership is lousy. This isn't an excuse for being an ineffective leader, but smart leaders can take advantage of the desire to belong.

People want to do more than work on a task. There-fore, as a leader, you need to build community among your team members. How can you help people get to know each other and develop friendships? What can you do to have fun in meetings? Creating an environ-ment where people enjoy each other is an important part of building a strong team. If the only thing that holds team members together is a task, they'll want to quit when work becomes difficult or unenjoyable.

Although most leaders are task-oriented, creating a sense of family and togetherness is important. Some leaders develop belonging with social activities or they create identity items such as matching shirts, logos, or embroidered caps. Creating a sense of togetherness with a common name, symbols and shared experiences is a powerful way for to help people fell like part of a team. Some go so far as to create secret handshakes, gestures and language.

Team Health

As a leader, you're also a bit of a parent. A good parent helps maintain a healthy home life. If you be-come a parent, you'll realize how difficult this can be. Even though you're not a parent to team members, you need to foster an emotionally positive family environ-ment. There will be personality differences, competing agendas, differing opinions, and conflicting values. How you handle these as a leader is vital to creating a healthy team. Do your members know why the team or organization exists? Can they state this in a single sentence? Sharing this common theme increases your team's sense of community and becomes a glue that sticks them together. Do the individuals on the team share the values of the team? If not, why not?

When people aren't getting along with each other, do you appear aloof and out of touch, or do you come on strong and try to intimidate people into pretending that they get along? Are you in tune with what it's like to be on the team? If so, on what do you base your belief?

As a leader, you're responsible for the health of the team, how they get along together and what it feels like to be a part of the organization. The primary purpose of leadership is to accomplish something together that we can't individually. Therefore, we all want to be a part of a team that stays on track. Leading a team is a lot like riding a horse. If you pull too hard on the reins, the horse won't go. If you give too much on the reins, the horse will gallop in any direction and end up losing the rider. Smart leaders know how to keep a balance on the team.

Common Problems

There are some common problems that leaders either don't see or fail to solve, in terms of creating team health:

- **Lack of affirmation:** We talked about this in Chapter 11 on giving and receiving effective feedback. But we want to bring it up again because this is important to team health. When people feel like they're being used, they'll resent it. Many leaders fail to understand the importance of saying, "thank you," "good job," and "we're so glad you're on this team." When leaders are too demanding or do not affirm team members, this affects the attitude of the team. Whether people are paid or not, shouldn't matter. When you affirm, try to be specific—"Jeff, I really like the e-mails you sent out to everyone before our meeting. That was terrific. Thanks for being on top of things. It really helped everyone show up on time." This is better than, "Josh, glad you're on the team." One of the most common criticisms that people have of their leaders is that they rarely affirm them—leaders ask, ask, ask without saying "thank you" and "great job."

• **Poor people skills:** A common problem in teams that don't get along well is unresolved anger. But a broader issue is poor people skills in general. When a leader isn't good at getting along with people, she's often out of touch with how team members are getting along. An ineffective leader allows people to fight, squabble and alienate each other within the group, often without being aware of it. She may wonder why people aren't happier during meetings or practices, but has no idea about the bickering going on in the locker room or in the parking lot after the meetings.

- **No fun:** There's an old saying, "All work and no play makes Jack a dull boy." You know what it's like to be young. You like to have fun. Sometimes, as people get older they forget how to have fun. They get consumed with work, bills, and life in general. As a young leader, you'll need to figure out how you can either combine fun with the task or in other ways.

The bottom line is that teams by nature are goal driven. Therefore, if you don't keep a purpose in front of your team, chances are it will become unhealthy. If you don't have a goal, either formal or informal, you're really not a team and therefore you don't need a leader. But if you're a leader working with people to accomplish something, you'll want to include some fun. Whether it's having a meal together; going out for ice cream after a meeting; or going to the beach, coffee shop, or park to play volleyball, be sure you weave in fun. Good leaders know they must focus on the task, but if you're only doing that, you won't be effective at leading, because people want to enjoy each other in the process.

Social Banking

Imagine leadership as a bank. When you establish an account with a bank, you begin a relationship where you can deposit and withdraw money. If you want to buy something, you take out money. If you want to take out money, you need to have put some into your account in the first place.

The same is true in relationships. As a leader, you're establishing a social bank account with people on your team. Because of your credibility, the fact that they like you and perhaps that you asked them to be on your team, you have emotional deposits into your account. When you compliment team members, thank them for their work, and use their ideas, the balance of your account increases. When a leader has a large enough deposit, he can make withdrawals. The size of the deposit required depends on the follower. Some require less; others more. This is when the leader asks the team member to do something, whether it's to attend a meeting, work on a task, or give up time and money for the cause. When you help your team succeed, you'll have more and more deposits, allowing you to withdraw more and more from your team. This is the emotional cycle of social banking in leadership.

But if you're too demanding; ask your team to make large sacrifices; or are generally negative, critical and fail to affirm your members, the balance in your social bank account goes down quickly. After a while, people will stop attending meetings and following you because you've overdrawn your account. Now your ability to lead is frozen.

Sometimes, banks give credit to customers they trust. When a leader is new,, people usually provide "credit." They assume they'll be paid back later, emotionally speaking, if they choose to follow and work toward the cause. As we mentioned in the chapter on integrity, if a leader has been untrustworthy or lacks credibility, people won't follow.

Often, leaders can't figure out why people have stopped following them or no longer seem committed. If this is your case, chances are you've overdrawn your account and need to make more deposits before requiring more from your team.

At the same time, leaders who make constant deposits but never withdraw are not good leaders. They like to be liked, but they don't get a lot done. A smart leader knows when to deposit and when to withdraw, so that she can accomplish things. If you never ask your team to do difficult things, you're wasting leadership.

An important role of a leader is to help people feel like they belong, that they're a part of a team. When leaders do this well, members are more motivated than normal. This emotional glue raises the level of commitment. Making sure people are treating each other fairly, getting along and enjoying themselves can be as important as concentrating on the task of the team itself.

Leader Reflections:

1. Describe a team you've been on that was fun or had strong unity.

2. Describe a team that was not fun to be on or where people didn't get along well.

3. Analyze these two teams and explain the differences. What role did the leader play in these two examples?

4. What do you think is fun in terms of team building/creating a unified team?

CHAPTER 22

COMMUNICATION

Start with Your Audience

Every leader is a communicator. When communication fails, leadership fails. What other way do you have to explain your vision, brainstorm and strategy than by communicating? I've taught communication for years and teach it in my work with military leaders at the Naval Postgraduate School. No matter how good you are, you can get better. I amaze myself with how inadequate I am at times, even though I teach, write and speak on the subject. The reason is because I'm dealing with humans, which makes good communication a difficult process.

As a leader, you have information, a vision, or opinion, and you want to get your ideas across to someone who may not have as much understanding of what you're talking about. What seems like basic information to you may not be to someone else. There are different personalities, thinking styles, and any number of competing issues that add to the situation.

But the main reason leaders fail is because they start in the wrong place. They begin with themselves or the message, instead of the audience. The most important principle of every type of communication is this: Start with your audience. Who are you trying to persuade? Who are you informing? What is your audience like? How do they like to receive communication —in person, by text, e-mail, Skype, in writing, or by phone? Are they older, younger, male, female, educated, uneducated, busy, or not? There are hundreds of qualities that make up the people you're trying to communicate with, so the better you know them, the more effective you'll be as a leader.

Research shows that leaders think they do a better job of communicating than they do. One of the biggest misperceptions is about how much they listen. More than 80 percent of leaders think they listen well. But when you survey people on their teams, only 17 percent of people think their leaders listen well. That means you need to do four times the amount of listening and clarifying than you think to match what you believe you're doing.

When leaders communicate poorly, people fill in the blanks with information that can be disastrous. When it's foggy in the mind of the leader, it will be very cloudy in team members' mind. What is it that makes a leader a good communicator?

Strive for Five

Here's a list of five things that will significantly improve your communication quotient:

1. **Listen more than you talk.** That's right. Communicating makes you think your job is about talking a lot, but it's not. Effective leaders listen more than they speak. The older I get, the less talking I do in group settings where I'm leading. I used to dominate meetings, thinking that was my job as leader. I've come to realize that hearing team members, getting their input, and allowing healthy discussion go a long way. Listening helps you understand what your teammates are thinking. It lets you know what they're worried about, unclear on, and excited to see happen. Until you listen effectively, you'll tend to miscommunicate, saying things that either don't make sense or lack the ability to inspire others. People are far more likely to hear what a leader has to say after the leader has listened to them. It's similar to research that proves people are more likely to buy a product after they've received a sample or gift from the seller.

2. **Learn to speak effectively.** Speaking is the single most important communication method for leading. That means you'll want to practice speaking. Toastmasters International is a club where people gather to improve their speaking skills. Although these groups typically consist of professionals, teens and college-age people can participate. You also can video yourself making a presentation, and then watch it. Take a public-speaking class in school, even if you don't need it for credit. When you make a speech, begin by answering this question, "Why should I listen to you?" If you don't do this well, you won't get their attention. If you don't have their attention, you can't communicate well.

3. **Learn to write well.** Chances are you're smart and talented, but if you write poorly, people will think you aren't. You may say, "I don't care what people think about me," but you should. If people don't think you're fairly smart and knowledgeable, they won't want to follow you. You may dislike writing in school, but it will help you be a better leader because leaders use writing as a tool for conveying their ideas to others. Whether it's a letter, e-mail, or job application, people will judge you based on your ability to communicate. This may not seem fair, but it's true. Practice grammar, spelling, sentence construction, and getting to your point using fewer words. If you don't succeed at first, keep trying. I always wanted to be an author, but in college one of my English teachers said I wasn't a very good writer. At first I was

very discouraged. Then I got angry. I improved. Since then, I've had the opportunity to have more than a dozen books and hundreds of articles published and was the executive editor of a national magazine.

4. **Clarify what others are hearing.** Just because you say or write something, that doesn't mean you've communicated. If written, is it compelling enough to be read? Have you stated the purpose quickly so people know what it's about and whether or not they need to or want to read it? Then there's the issue of "did they hear what you meant for them to hear?" The only way you can tell is by seeking clarification. "What do you think about that? How did that letter come across to you? What do you hear me saying?" Getting feedback is important, but, unfortunately, most leaders don't ask for it and even when they do many team members aren't honest because they either fear the leader or want to avoid hurting his feelings. Finding an honest friend who'll give you good feedback is valuable.

5. **Make it stick.** A "sticky" message stays with us; we don't forget it. It often includes an experience wrapped in an activity. Think creatively when it comes to designing your messages. Can you give your receivers something to do or a souvenir they can take with them after a meeting? Perhaps you create an activity that communicates your point. We use a lot of active learning in our LeadNow and LeadWell training programs because we know it's the

best way for people to remember what it is they've learned. Sticky messages aren't lectures or rambling e-mails. They leave people talking. Make your messages fun, interesting and attention-grabbing.

Communication is a very important tool for leading. Wars have started due to poor leader communication. Best friends have become enemies. The better a leader is at communicating, the more he or she can help the team stay on the task.

Leader Reflections:

1. What do you think is the most challenging part of communicating?

2. Can you think of a time when you or another leader communicated poorly? What went wrong?

3. Why do you think the audience is the most important part of effective communicating?

4. Write a three-minute speech on a topic you like that will allow you to get feedback from others.

CHAPTER 23

CONFLICT

Unmet Expectations

One of the most challenging factors of any leadership process is conflict, putting out relational fires. No one enjoys it when team members don't get along with each other or when they feel irritated toward you, the leader. Conflict primarily occurs when people have unmet expectations. Perhaps the expectation was to do a task a certain way. When their way wasn't selected, they got mad. Another expectation may be having a certain role on a team. They also feel frustrated when they don't receive affirmations and rewards, or when they feel their time isn't being valued. Unmet expectations vary from person to person because you're bringing individuals together who've given up some of their preferences to be a part of a team.

When people are unwilling to change their expectations, they feel resentful. This resentment affects team chemistry, causing the team to be less effective. That's when a leader steps in because her job is to help the team be productive. Here are some practical ways to deal with conflict:

1. **Identify conflict.** Sometimes leaders think they don't have conflict because people aren't fighting or arguing. This isn't necessarily true. When people aren't sharing their differences of opinion, the cause may be passive-aggressive behavior. This is when people get back at you in ways that don't appear to be violent or obvious, but the team suffers. Let's say that Benji is mad because he didn't get his way in a recent meeting, but his personality is more reserved and quiet, so instead of getting angry or telling you his frustration, Benji decides to not respond to your e-mails or phone calls. He starts showing up late to meetings, and after he arrives, sends texts while others are talking. Although he's never told you he's upset, this is his way of getting back at you or other team members.

Passive-aggressive behavior is just as much conflict as two people arguing. It can actually be worse because it can go undetected. People may not tell you what's wrong or merely answer, "Nothing," when you ask, "Is everything OK?" Leaders need to be good at reading people, understanding their body language, facial expressions, and the tone of their voice. This gives you cues that help you know whether or not people are agreeing with you.

2. **Assess the intensity of conflict.** You may find it helpful to rate conflict you see on a 1–5 scale:

- **Level 1** is very minor, petty, and is often more personal. Quite often, you can overlook this when you're a leader. Maybe someone is just in a bad mood or tired.

- **Level 2** is minor, meaning someone had a different opinion about a solution or felt irritated that the meeting started 10 minutes late. A leader may or may not want to address this level of conflict. If it's ongoing, a leader may want to talk to the person or persons. Fixing the problem may be easy.

- **Level 3** is significant, meaning that one or more people are upset enough to negatively impact meetings and relationships outside the team. At this level, a leader may want to meet individually with the people involved to better understand the situation.

- **Level 4** is very significant. Unresolved issues of this intensity will shake the team apart if left un-managed. A leader must assertively interact with the people involved and, if possible, get them to meet together to resolve their issues. If their anger is toward you as the leader, you'll want to have someone neutral help everyone process it. You also want to be sure you aren't misquoted and that people don't gang up against you. The faster you can address a Level 4 conflict, the better.

- **Level 5** is severe, meaning that people have started physically fighting or are so angry that they're quitting the team, badmouthing to others about your leadership, or intentionally trying to divide the team. Leaders must act quickly. A Level 3 that is ignored can catch fire and escalate to a Level 4 or Level 5.

Leaders are like firemen, trying to put out a flame before it becomes large. Like a fireman, you don't pull the fire alarm when a person strikes a match or lights a candle. That's why assessing the level of conflict is important. If you overreact, you'll scare your team and they'll shut down, hiding their potential conflicts. How you handle a conflict is just as important as *if* you handle it. Ineffective leaders frequently make situations worse by failing to address conflicts or handling them in the wrong way. Many parents yell at their arguing kids, "Knock it off, or I'll knock it off for you!" This isn't very effective. The same is true of leaders.

3. **Resolve the conflict.** You don't have to have a degree in psychology or be a professional counselor to help your team manage their conflicts. When conflict exists between other team members, your job is to help them talk about it. You may need to do a little work beforehand and meet with each party. Gaining perspective on each person's frustration is important. Establishing ground rules is also helpful, such as, "We want to focus on the issue, not people," "We want to let the other person finish speaking before we respond," and "We want to honor each other even though we disagree." These are examples of fighting fair. You can come back to these after you've set the guidelines with whomever you're meeting.

If the conflict is between you and another person, it's your responsibility as leader to initiate contact, even if it's the other person's problem—"Jamie, it seems like we're not connecting like we used to. Is there something I've done that's hurt you? What can we do to resolve this? I want to make this right if I can." These are great statements to begin a conversation, because often people feel intimidated by leaders or they feel that you'll use your position against them.

If someone has an issue with you as the leader, it's your responsibility to discuss it. This is difficult because you're human. Keeping your emotions stable while trying to listen and be a good leader isn't easy—you need the skin of a rhinoceros and the heart of a lamb. Leaders know what it's like to be criticized and want to defend themselves, tell critics what they think, and shoot down others' opinions. But leaders who do this become dictators, despots and tyrants. We want to be different, don't we? We want to be really good at handling conflict and different views so we can tap the potential of the team and not alienate people in the process.

Conflict Is Good and Bad

Identifying and estimating the level of conflict is important, but so is realizing when conflict is good. That's right, conflict is also a part of effective teams and organizations. People who analyze organizations say that some conflict is helpful. When there isn't enough conflict, the organization is not being productive and people feel controlled and therefore negative.

Conflict is also good when...

• People openly discuss their frustrations.

• Differing opinions bring new ideas.

- People feel they matter.

- Leaders hear what they need to improve about their leading.

  Conflict is bad when...

- People are shot down and not allowed to talk about their concerns.

- Leaders fail to jump in, and people are hurt in the process.

- It derails the team from its primary task.

- Leaders don't allow conflict with them to help them improve.

As you practice these skills of conflict management, you'll become respected as a leader, even among your enemies. People who disagree with you will have good things to say about you if you're fair, kind and willing to honor people, even when you disagree with them. Keeping this sort of peace on the team is important. While you'll never resolve all conflict, your ability to manage it well is vital to great leading.

Leader Reflections:

1. What is it you dislike most about conflict?

2. Describe a situation when a leader did a poor job handling conflict.

3. Describe a situation when a leader did a great job managing conflict.

4. What conflict-handling skill do you want to work on as a leader?

CHAPTER 24

POWER

Power: Fear and Embrace It

Most of the time when leaders make news in a big way, it's because they've misused their power. Power is leadership muscle. When leaders make bad ethical decisions and when they lack integrity, power is what makes them think they can do what they want, that no one can stop them, and that they can get away with what they shouldn't. Some leaders kill people. Others have them killed. Other leaders take bribes, steal money from their organizations, cheat on their mates, and tell lies to cover up their bad deeds. Even though people without power can do wrong, when leaders do it, many more suffer. So if power is dangerous, why should we seek it as leaders?

The reason is if you don't have power, you can't lead. There's no such thing as a powerless leader. When you have no power, you're no longer leading. That's what makes leadership so difficult. You need to get power to lead, but power is also dangerous. It tempts us to do things we shouldn't, because we think we can.

Sometimes people say that leaders shouldn't seek power. While that sounds nice, it's not true. What most people mean is leaders shouldn't seek power for their own good. When leaders become "power hungry" or "power mongers," they're using power in selfish and hurtful ways. We want good leaders to get power because they help people. They make sure others are treated well. They accomplish much good through their leading. When good people have less power than bad people, bad people win because it's not who is right who wins, but who has the most power.

These are strong statements to be telling you, but you need to know how leadership works. This is the dark side of leading that gets a bad reputation, and it should. When leaders use power selfishly and to hurt others, everyone eventually loses.

That's why we want people like you to use power in a good way. When you learn how leadership works and become a leader in your school, community, organization, and eventually in companies and countries, many will benefit. When more good people learn how to get and use power well, the better our world will be.

Power Sources

Gaining power may be one of the most important things you can do to speed up the process of gaining influence as a young leader. For the most part, young leaders lack impact because they lack power. For the most part, leadership is about adults who are employed by companies, governments, and organizations that expect them to use their education, skills and experience to bring about change. Some of this is an age issue, but some of it is simply because society doesn't trust young leaders and therefore avoids giving power to them. But at the same time, young leaders lack power because they don't understand how to acquire it. Actually, there are multiple sources where you can obtain power for leading. Here are the six primary ones:

- **Position:** Obviously, the president of the United States has a lot more power than the person who merely ran for the office. Certain positions have more power than others when they're in organizations. This is what we refer to as formal power, also known as authority. A lot of people assume this is the only way to get power for leading, but it isn't.

- **People:** Knowing people with influence can give you power. Let's say your uncle is the CEO of a big company. Because you know him, he can open doors of opportunity for you, such as introducing you to other people in his industry when you need a job, or even an old college friend who is president of a university you want to attend. Who you know is a powerful resource for young leaders, but also consider who knows who you know.

- **Talent/Skill:** Steve Jobs (founder of Apple), Mark Zuckerberg, (founder of Facebook), and Steven Spielberg (movie producer) are examples of leaders who gained power primarily from their talent and skill. They're exceptional at what they did/do, so much so that they've been able to build large organizations. You can have a talent or skill and not be a leader. For example, you can be a great soccer player and not be able to lead, but if you have an ability to lead, you can use a strong talent of playing basketball to become your team captain and perhaps later a great coach.

- **Resources:** This source can be muscle (i.e., physical strength), equipment (e.g., military), land, buildings, money, or time. These tend to be things you possess. Leaders who are able to acquire certain resources become very powerful. You can also combine who you know with the resources they have, in the hope you can access these resources.

- **Information:** Knowing certain things gives you a power that those without it don't possess. This can be formal education, information about a person or subject, or access to answers that can be used to influence people. Even today, bad leaders try to control information that people get, such as when rulers shut off the Internet, because information can empower people.

• **Personality:** This may be the most difficult power source to obtain because it has more to do with the type of personality you have. Charisma refers to the ability to impress us with great people skills, along with confidence, charm, and making others feel special when they're around you. Although charisma is often overrated, and those who rely too heavily on it can get others to follow them even when they have nowhere to go, charisma and the ability to communicate are powerful influence resources.

Power is an important part of leading, but, like electricity, social power can be a dangerous thing if not used properly. But good leaders aren't afraid of power and use it for the good of people. They realize that without it they can't do a lot. People who aren't ethical may use power for evil. A leader without power isn't a strong leader. He or she can't accomplish much. Smart leaders know how to obtain it and realize there are multiple ways to find it, not just one. Don't complain because you're young and powerless. This is victim talk and is an excuse used by people who can't figure out how to get things done creatively and by tapping into other power sources.

Leader Reflections:

1. Why do you think power tends to be thought of negatively?

2. List three to four leaders you know and describe the type(s) of power they possess.

3. How do these leaders use their power?

4. What are some power sources you might have that you haven't considered?

CHAPTER 25

VISION

A Preferred Future

Vision may be the most difficult of the 16 leadership qualities to explain, because it's a lot like art. When you see a beautiful painting, it inspires you, but it's difficult to describe. If you're not artistic, it's not easy to learn how to create art. Vision to a leader is what a sculpture or painting is to an artist. A vision is more felt than thought.

A vision is a preferred future. A leader looks ahead of the rest, to see what is possible.

Determining and communicating the vision is primarily the leader's responsibility. This involves making decisions, choosing words, images and emotions that motivate people to pursue that vision. A manager sets a goal—a leader casts a vision. Throughout history, visions have inspired people to take action, make personal sacrifices, and change what they were planning to do. When a leader shares her vision, it's more than just a goal or plan; it has more to do with helping people find their purpose in her leading and why they need to accomplish whatever it is the leader states as the mission. A vision moves the heart as much as the head. Many of the great speeches throughout history have been vision speeches. (A great place to find American speeches is at www.americanrhetoric.com.)

The word *vision* is great because it's about seeing, creating a mental picture of what it is we want to achieve as a team or organization. When a leader doesn't have a mental picture of what he wants his team to achieve, others will lack motivation and be unsure of what it is they're trying to accomplish.

Of all the leadership qualities we teach, vision is the most difficult because we've found that it's more caught then taught and more intuitive than learned. Even though we've found it difficult to teach, we've analyzed enough vision speeches to notice ingredients that make them visionary.

Measuring a Vision

Certain ingredients make a chocolate chip cookie great. Similarly, specific elements make a vision effective. Here are the key components you can look for in analyzing your vision and other visions to see how effective they may be in motivating others to follow you:

- **Importance:** Why do we need to pursue this project? What difference will it make if we achieve it, or if we don't? Why do we need to win this game, defeat the opponent, or accomplish this goal? If a vision lacks importance, people won't prioritize it. If it won't change lives or leave a mark in history, why waste our time and energy? When you create a vision statement, emphasize the bigger picture. "We need to recycle our garbage because we must do our part to save our earth," instead of "We need to recycle because our waste management company expects us to do it."

- **Urgency:** Importance isn't enough because if people can procrastinate, they often will. There are a lot of things people believe are important that most don't do, like exercising, eating healthy and recycling. The reason is a lack of urgency. I spoke with John Kotter, a former professor at Harvard University and expert on leadership and organizational change. He said the main reason organizations fail to change is they lack a sense of urgency. Why do we need to do this now? Why is this a unique opportunity? Why is time of the essence? This helps people prioritize the vision over other things competing for their attention.

- **Size:** How big is the vision? Is it about changing the world or merely putting toner in the printer? If you want people to recycle their garbage, a vision will focus on being a part of saving the world, not just putting more recycling bins in classrooms. A practical vision results in strategies and goals, but it's bigger than these. Large visions inspire people far more than little ones. Be sure you tap into the greater idea of mission, purpose, destiny and changing society.

- **Clarity:** What do you want us to do? Be clear. If it's muddy in your mind as the leader, it'll be even muddier in others' minds. This isn't just a cheer to get people excited. A vision is an inspiring blueprint to show us where we're headed and specifically what you want us to do as team members. We must be able to "do" the vision, so being clear is important. Far too many vision statements lack clarity, so motivated people become frustrated because they want to get involved, but don't know what to do. Eventually, people stop following leaders who lack clarity. Here's an example of a simple vision statement for an athletic team: "The vision of our team is to play to the best of our ability and to win as many games possible through hard work, unity, and a desire to win."

- **Intensity:** One last factor is what I call the fuel that drives a vision speech. By "speech" I mean something as formal as a presentation by a national leader or something as simple as a leader trying to get his buddies to do something together. When I studied the psychology of communication in my graduate program in college, I investigated what specifically made some speakers great and others only average. Although a vision can be communicated in many ways, including media clips, posters, and such, leader speeches are primary. Of all the factors that make a speech great, intensity is the single one that creates magic in communicating. By intensity, we mean how passionate the speaker is about the subject. It can be evidenced in the eyes, the inflection of the voice, and the energy the speaker exudes. If the leader isn't passionate about and committed to his vision, others won't be either. Although intensity alone won't carry a vision, a vision speech lacking intensity rarely inspires others to significant commitment.

Coming up with a leadership vision is more "caught than taught." It has to do with what you feel in your heart and imagine in your head. Painting a mental picture for others to see what your team can accomplish is what leaders do best. Although we've not really taught you how to "do" vision in this chapter, think of what you've read as you watch the vision speeches on the Internet that we've recommended, as well as leaders you hear giving small or large speeches. The leader's goal is to persuade people to take action, join a cause, and pursue something important. Remember, a vision doesn't need to be delivered in a formal presentation. It can be done one on one over coffee. It could be as simple as someone in the cafeteria convincing her friends to go to a certain event next weekend. Look for the qualities we discussed. Try to replicate these in your leading, so people will be inspired to follow you, join your team, and then climb whatever mountain you're scaling.

Leader Reflections:

1. Describe a leader you're familiar with who seems to do a good job communicating a vision.

2. Watch a few of the suggested video clips (www. americanrhetoric.com) and analyze them in terms of the vision factors of importance, urgency, size, clarity, and intensity. Which of these got your attention? What about the vision inspired you?

3. Try writing a short vision speech you can give about a topic you feel is important.

CHAPTER 26

STRATEGY

Designing a Plan

A vision is where we want to be. But to get from where we are to where we want to be requires strategy. A vision that has no plan is like a helium balloon without a string to hold it to the ground. The balloon floats into the sky, never to be seen again. While vision is the helium, the string that keeps it within reach is the plan. Vision is about why and what; strategic planning is about how and when. The order goes like this: vision → strategy → plan → action.

Leading doesn't always require an inspiring vision. Sometimes you just need to direct an event or solve a crisis. But nearly everything a leader does requires some sort of strategy. Imagine a trip from your home to a specific address in Hong Kong. You can select multiple ways to get there. Some people have airline options, each with a different time and cost. Most would need a passport. Then there's land transportation (bus, taxi, car, train or bicycle). Is the strategy to get there quickly, inexpensively, or safely? The strategy often determines the best option, and this determines your plan.

Strategizing is the process of figuring out how to accomplish the goal. The more complicated a goal is, the more difficult it becomes to establish a suitable strategy. The best leaders don't do this alone. They use the ideas and resources of the team. The leader's primary role in strategizing is to help the team discover options and possibilities, determine the best one, and then implement it. These ideas come from teammates and outside sources; you don't have to find them yourself as the leader.

I learned a valuable leader lesson during an executive training program hosted by the Center for Creative Leadership. My team picked me to be the team leader for an exercise to get our team across a river of hot lava with limited resources. (The lava was pretend, by the way.) I'm not very good at engineering or mechanical thinking, but I was certain someone else would be better at this task, so I passed up leading to another person. After the activity was over, the team told me that I shouldn't have given up leading just because I didn't have the best answers. The leader's job is to help uncover them, not to find them alone.

Common Young Leader Errors

Over the last few years of working with 100s of young and very young leaders, we've identified trends of errors that young leaders make more than older leaders. Obviously, much of this has to do with life experience and learning from our mistakes, but if you can avoid some of these failures, you'll be far ahead of the rest.

- **Jumping in before thinking:** This is common when young leaders who lack experience feel under a lot of pressure to just start doing something. Whenever possible, push a mental "pause" button and think about how it is you want to lead. What's the best style for this situation? How am I going to approach this problem? These are all questions you may want to ponder before you begin. If you don't have time to step back and think through your approach, you can gain time by opening the process up to others' ideas and then using your influence as a leader to change direction if you decide to go a different direction.

- **Settling for good instead of great:** While developing young leaders around the world, I've noticed a tendency to settle for a less than best strategy. When one person comes up with a strategic idea that seems sensible, the leader jumps on it instead of exploring the possibilities. Saying, "OK, let's do it," interrupts the brainstorm process that could uncover better ideas. Even quick brainstorms can usually result in multiple strategies that vary in quality. As much as possible, develop several strategies so you don't stop at the first good one your team develops.

- **Failing to listen well:** Leaders often think their job is to take over solving problems. They start telling people what to do instead of listening for ideas, opinions and feedback. When you rush people or shoot them down, you reduce the chance that they'll share again. If the main voice heard in meetings is yours, chances are, you're reducing the effectiveness of your leading.

- **Falling victim to analysis paralysis:** Another common error we see among young leaders is taking too long to analyze options and get ready. Naturally, strategizing has to consider the amount of time available, but when a leader takes too long to get going, you may lose valuable opportunities. Sometimes this is because leaders fear making a decision; other times it's because they fail to focus on the clock. Pacing the strategizing process isn't easy. There comes a time when the leader must decide.

- **Allowing hijacking:** Hijacking is a term we use when a stronger or louder leader takes over for a less confident or quieter leader. When you see team members taking over your responsibility of leading, you need to step up your participation as well as push back on the other leader—"Tim, thanks for sharing these ideas, but I'm leading this meeting. I appreciate your help, but I need your help in letting me lead right now." Power struggles are common among leaders, but if you let another leader take over, others won't trust you, nor will the hijacker. People hijack for various reasons. Sometimes they're stronger leaders; other times it's because they haven't learned self-control. Although they may seem strong, hijackers often need direct communication. That means you need to increase your leadership involvement.

- **Getting distracted by the task:** The leader's primary job is to focus on the team and help it stick to the strategy. When the leader gets distracted by the task, she has a difficult time seeing how the rest of the team is doing and if the strategy is working. Young leaders tend to become preoccupied by the task itself. They enjoy doing instead of stepping back and helping the team do the task.

- **Being satisfied with OK results:** A common habit of young leaders is feeling satisfied with modest results, instead of thinking how the team can improve. To get better, you'll need to re-strategize. What's working? What isn't? How can we improve? What can we do to get better? What's another way of doing this?

Is it better? How can we be more productive? Who's doing well and who isn't? A leader is always observing the strategy and seeing what can be improved on as a team, as well as asking for feedback. Even when you're winning, is there a way to get better? Chances are, there is, if you re-strategize. Instead of merely improving the existing strategy, is there a different approach we might take?

Strategizing is an important part of leading. There are rarely single strategies for solving problems. Getting from one place to another with a team requires a lot of energy and good thinking by the leader. Gaining experience from practice, rehearsal, observing others, reading, studying, and asking for advice are all ways to use the best information when strategizing.

Leader Reflections:

1. Describe a leader you know who is good at strategizing. What makes this person effective to you?

2. What do you think is the most difficult part of strategizing?

3. Which of the young leader weaknesses have you seen?

4. Come up with some other ways to respond to people who try to hijack a meeting or plan that you're leading.

CHAPTER 27

CHANGE

Transitions

Leadership is about helping people change. A person who is managing a team or organization is primarily keeping things the way they are. You're not changing a lot. Managing is important, but it's different than leading. Leading requires you to go over or around challenges that block your way.

One thing that makes leading difficult is most people don't enjoy change. They like things the way they've been. You may have heard the phrase "creature of habit." Researchers suggest that 80 percent of people resist change by nature. That's one of the main reasons why leading is difficult, because you're asking people to do something different. You're challenging them to change. It may involve an adjustment in their actions. For some, the transition means giving up time and money; for others, you're trying to transform their lives. Don't underestimate how difficult it is to lead people through change.

To do that, you must be flexible. People who are rigid and unable to respond emotionally to a change of plans or circumstances usually don't make good leaders. Let's say that you're planning a big outdoor event with food, activities and games. On the weekend of the event, there's a big rainstorm. How are you going to handle it? Do you cancel the event? Is there a backup plan? Do people attending the event know where to go? What about all the people responsible for the tents, food and activities; do they know what to do? Dozens of decisions will need to be made quickly in response to the storm.

Your ability to respond to create a flexible plan is an important leader quality. People will be looking for you to lead them during these times, all while remaining calm and hopeful. Coming up with alternative ideas quickly is a test of a true leader.

Organizational Life Span

An organization, by its very nature, tries to stay the same. It's a survival mechanism that most living things possess. Our physical bodies do that. They try to reject germs and influences that attempt to change them. That's why sometimes, when a person gets an organ transplant, the body rejects the very thing it needs. Change is difficult because organizations try to stay the same. They naturally reject things that try to disrupt the way they are.

But to survive, organizations eventually need to change. Following is a graphic we refer to as an *S* curve, because it looks like the letter *S*. This curve reflects how an organism or organization begins, grows, and eventually becomes stale and dies.

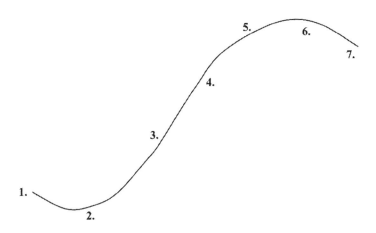

- **Point #1** is the start of a new idea. This is exciting. Something new is about to happen. A vision is inspiring.

- **Point #2** is when you start the idea and things get tough. People realize it'll be work or that they'll have to give up something. They wonder if it's worth it.

- **Point #3** is when you begin seeing some progress. You start thinking that in spite of the hard work, it may be worth it.

- **Point #4** is when you gain momentum and people feel things are going well. They see success coming. You begin adding structure and stability.

- **Point #5** is when the team or organization is productive. At this point, it's tempting to sit back and relax—"Ah, we've made it." But effective leaders know that this is the time when they need to be thinking of new ideas and improvements. Everyone else seems happy, but the leader is thinking ahead. If not, the organization moves to point #6 and beyond.

- **Point #6** is when things begin to taper off and lose momentum. No one feels fearful yet, but things aren't as they were.

- **Point #7** is when decline is evident to most people. Leaders find it very difficult to bring about change now because they've lost momentum. Turnaround becomes difficult. Past this point, very few organizations change; most die. Often it's easier to start something new.

Although this is a fast explanation, young leaders need to understand how organizations function, as well as people. Where the organization is on the *S*-curve will determine how difficult the change will be.

Nelson Change Formula

Over the years, I've studied a lot about organizational change. As a result, I've developed a formula for understanding how various factors work together and to estimate the difficulty of change. Most leaders are never trained in how to bring about organizational change. Over the years, I've read most books on this topic and have developed a formula that helps leaders estimate how difficult a change process will be. We won't go into the details of how these factors work together here, but let me introduce the four main factors:

1. **Leader Umph:** This is the strength of the leader. The stronger the leader, the easier it is to bring about change, because people feel confident in the leader and trust him or her. The weaker the leader, the more difficult it'll be to bring about change.

2. **Influencer Readiness:** Think about the other people with influence in the organization. Then consider whether they are for or against the change idea. The more who are for it, the easier change will be. The more who are against it, the more difficult the change will be.

3. **Time:** The less time you have, the more difficult change will be. The larger the organization, the longer change takes. A group of friends can change very quickly, but a school, community, or big company may take a few years to change.

4. **Idea Impact:** How different will the organization be when the new idea is implemented? Will it affect the organization a lot, or will people hardly notice it? The bigger the impact, the more difficult change will be; the smaller the impact, the easier it will be.

These four factors work together and can give you an estimate of how difficult change will be. Most leaders underestimate how difficult change is, so they underprepare and then get frustrated when things don't go as they hope.

Team Member Change

One thing you'll want to consider when you lead is what kind of change you're expecting from the team members. For example, on a sports team the leader realizes that to become a great team, members need to get into physical shape. Therefore, you may need to ask people to come early and stay late to exercise and lift weights. You may have to ask certain players to change the position they prefer playing because you think it'll make a stronger team.

As a part of the team, leaders need to change as well. An effective leader asks, "What do I need to do to change?" That's an important question because experts say that before an organization can change, the leader must change. This may mean changing the way you lead, recruiting better people, giving others authority, or stepping back from trying to do too much. It's tempting to look at others and see what you want to be different without looking at yourself and seeing where you may be part of the problem. Personal change is required of the leader for the organization to change.

As a leader, you'll want to be flexible. If you're set in your ways, you'll have a lot of trouble leading other people who are likely to also be stuck in their ways. One benefit you have as a young leader is that as people get older they often become more resistant to change. While you're young, you're more likely to take risks, try new things, and be dissatisfied with the way things are. That's good. Use that energy to bring about change as a leader. Help people see what can be. Patiently assist them in moving out of their comfort zone and embracing the new. Do it with honor and compassion, because you're asking people to do a difficult thing, to give up what is familiar.

Leader Reflections:

1. What's something you'd like to change about your school or an organization you know?

2. Why do you think people in this organization haven't tried to change? If they've tried, why did they fail?

3. What do you find exciting, scary, or difficult about change?

4. What do you think about the idea that the leader needs to change along with or even before the organization?

WRAP-UP

Congratulations on reading this book! You're already significantly further than your peers, who typically won't read a book on leading until their late twenties or thirties. This isn't everything you'll need to know about leading, but the material you've just read will impact nearly every leadership situation you'll find yourself in as a leader. The cool thing is that you're a young leader. By gaining experience and working on the concepts in this book, you're off to a great start.

I believe in you. I'm convinced that the greatest leaders have yet to live because we've not taken young leaders seriously. We overlook them and treat them like kids or wannabe leaders—"Someday, you're going to be a leader," they say, patting you on the head. Well, that someday is now. If you're wired to lead, there's no reason you need to wait until your thirties, forties, or fifties to do significant things. You can use influence now to help people work together to accomplish what they couldn't as individuals. I'm proud of you. Please e-mail me (alan@kidlead.com) and let me know how this book has helped you, how I can improve it, and how our organization can help you take your leading to the next level. Our LeadWell training curriculum is for 14- to 18-year-olds and the LeadStrong program is for ages 19 to 25.

The world is going to be a better place because of your influence. Use it to improve what you do in helping people. Join us at www.leadyoung.org.

Lead now, lead well, and lead strong!

IF NOT NOW, WHEN?
IF NOT YOU, WHO?

—Hillel